VOLUME 3 OF THE ESSENTIAL LATINO PLAYS SERIES

LATINOLOGUES & MÁS MONOLOGUES

BY RICK L. NAJERA

WPR BOOKS: LATINO INSIGHTS

CARLSBAD, CA

DEDICATION

This collection of monologues is dedicated to a brave
16-year-old Mexican-American girl who got on a train from
Boone, Iowa, and came to California to follow her dreams.

THE BOOK CREATIVE TEAM
Layout & Design: Katharine A. Díaz
Cover Illustration: Momo Rodriguez
Editorial Assistant: Susie Albin-Najera
Publisher: Kirk Whisler

For more about books presented by WPR Publishing, please go to www.
WPRbooks.com.

WPR BOOKS: Latino Insights
3445 Catalina Dr., Carlsbad, CA 92010-2856
www.WPRbooks.com 760-434-1223 kirk@whisler.com

TABLE OF CONTENTS

Rick Najera's
LATINOLOGUES

MONOLOGUES ABOUT LATINO LIFE IN AMERICA

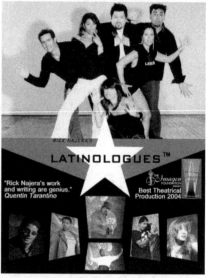

LATINOLOGUES™ & MÁS MONOLOGUES

PLAYWRIGHT'S NOTES

From the barrio to Broadway and back, the comedic stage play *Latinologues*™ has shared the struggles and the hilarity of Latino culture and metamorphosed into something bigger than I ever imagined.

When I first came to LA and began to write TV shows, I began to notice a lack of casting for Latinos in Hollywood. So I created *Latinologues* to be more of a showcase for actors including myself.

In the beginning . . . *Latinologues* began as my own personal protest against Prop 187, the harsh, anti-illegal alien bill denying basic services and healthcare rights. In lieu of Latinos rioting, as some claimed might happen if this bill passed, I wanted to explain Latinos through humor and provide insight to my culture. Ironically, today there are harsher laws against Latinos in this country in Georgia and Arizona to name a few and unfortunately more to come.

The first production was at the Odyssey theatre in West Los Angeles in 1994 and performed with comedians Debi Gutierrez, Rudy Moreno, Gene Pompa and myself. Those comedians joined me on stage that first night years ago and now, with more than 150 actors rotating in the cast, the show is considered the longest running Latino-oriented showcase in America.

Each year that passed, I added more material and more monologues, and each year, the show grew and reached even larger audiences. The actors saw the benefits from performing in the show; several went on to Broadway like Carlos Gomez went on to star in *In the Heights*; Jesse Garcia went to *The Pee Wee Herman Show* and several went on to successful film careers.

In 2004, *Latinologues* caught the attention of producer Robin Tate when the show played to a sold-out house at the Spreckles Theatre in San Diego, leaving hundreds stranded outside without a ticket. Tate saw the potential then, as well as at the following sold-out show in New York at Townhall Theatre and decided to take the show to Broadway.

Latinologues made its Broadway debut in 2005 at the historic Helen Hayes Theater, next to legendary Broadway shows such as *Phantom of the Opera, Spamalot* and *Lennon*. The show was directed by comedy legend, Cheech Marin and starred a Puerto Rican (Shirley A. Rumerick) as well as a Cuban (Rene Lavan). It also starred a Mexican citizen (Eugenio Derbez) and a Mexican-American (myself). We invited guest actors to perform such as Jaime Camil, El Gordo (Raul de Molina) and rapper Unik to name a few. The play ran for 137 performances including previews and an extension. No other play that was written, produced, directed and starring Latinos had ever done that before. The show's successes began to make Latinos on Broadway a reality. *Latinologues* and John Leguizamo paved the way for Lin Manuel Miranda's *In the Heights*.

Latinologues has toured the country from Los Angles to New York to Miami and all the cities in between. The show was produced in some of the nation's regional theaters such as the South Coast Repertory Theatre and the San Diego Repertory Theater. It also ran at the New Jersey Performing Arts Center and many other venues. Featured on *Showtime's* Latino Laugh Festival, *Latinologues* has touched a collective nerve in America. The show has entertained a diverse and cultured audience from neighborhoods, clubs, and even alcohol—fueled crowds at the House of Blues in Chicago, Los Angeles and the Improv in Los Angeles. After 15 years, and after much demand, these memorable characters are now in a written format. after much demand.

I recall one particular evening where I played in a Chicago club. There was a "fight night." That's when they put a boxing ring in the middle of the club and amateurs from the crowd get a chance to fight for prize money. *Latinologues* was performed after that fight. It was, as we say in the hood, "ghettolicious." I heard a woman say as she stepped into the ring, "Hold my drink, bitch; and don't hit me in the stomach, I'm pregnant." Yes, we played to that crowd. Those were my "groundlings".

Throughout the years, this show has undergone much tweaking and updating, and I'm sure the play will continue to undergo more changes. Borrowed from the Comedia Del Arte style of relevant comedy and of topical humor. I was keenly aware of the audience that the show served.

The great white way was not so white when *Latinologues* came to Broadway. That has made me profoundly happy. It was a chance for Latinos to join the marketplace of Broadway and add their talent. Comedy was my mission, and being more of a populist writer, I cared many times more for my audience than for the critics. Luckily, the critics gave *Latinologues* fine reviews and they still do. But I always had the audience in mind and felt that if the general Anglo audience did not get it, they would in time. After all, I understood Jackie Mason when he played at the Helen Hayes Theater on Broadway. Only a few years before *Latinologues* played at that same theater, Jackie Mason was viewed as only a Catskills entertainer. He had become mainstream and one of my favorite writers. Mel Brooks went from film to Broadway. We are all in a cultural evolution. We are all evolving and the world is getting smaller, and that, in turn, demands that our spirits become larger as we embrace other cultures and change.

It was the first chance for many to see themselves on stage, and for me, one of the greatest moments I had was while on Broadway, I was eating at Sardi's restaurant on W. 44th. A busboy came up to me and said, "Thank you. I saw your show last night. You gave someone like me with no voice, a voice." I was stunned and humbled by the poetry of his words. Here was a busboy from Puebla, Mexico who saw a Broadway show about his life. I realized that plays and entertainment can be revolutionary and comedy can address social questions at times better than politicos.

My audiences seemed to be made up of many types. I remember once in Texas at the Alley Theater, a big white Texan wearing a Stetson hat came up to me. He said, "Hold on a minute. Can I tell you I really like your work?" My own prejudices thought he would not enjoy my work, but he did. I learn as much from my audiences as they learn from me. Our stories are Latino stories, but when you become specific, you can end up with a universal message.

L.–r.: Cheech Marin, Geraldo Rivera and Rick L. Najera at the opening-night party of Latinologues *on Broadway.*

One of my favorite quotes about the show came at the reception on opening night on Broadway, from Geraldo Rivera, who was sitting at our table along with Cheech Marin. He took out his pen and grabbed a napkin and wrote:

> *"My dad used to say that the only real difference between the various Latinos was the color of the beans. What Latinologues manages with humor and sharp insight is to capture the great culture and spirit we share in common. The rich tapestry is presented in clever, sharply written vignettes that made me roar with belly laughs born of familiarity. That's my family's story. I know that guy. This is our Fiddler. Funny, real, relevant, smart and did I say funny?"*

–Geraldo Rivera

What I have provided for you in this book is most closely based on the *Latinologues* performance run on Broadway, with the most recent renditions of the monologues performed at Los Angeles' Conga Room on September 2, 2010. By the time this goes to print, more venues will be added. I have also decided to include some of the most unforgettable characters that were not in the show as an appendage—just to spice it up a bit and sprinkle a little extra Latin love. I hope you enjoy this comedy *caldo* (soup)—and remember that all these characters were born from real people I met or based sometimes on Latino stereotypes that I wanted to overturn. They are our stories; they are *Latinologues*.

Included in the anthology of my work are additional monologues performed in various incarnations of *Latinologues—Más Monologues* and *Buford Gomez*, a one-man show performed in Texas. But the show is now and will always be a chance for Latino actors and actresses to add their own interpretations. I hope you enjoy my work as much as I have enjoyed creating it.

—Rick L. Najera

Photo by Oscar Toruno

Latinologues cast backstage at the Hayworth theater (l.–r.):
Rick L. Najera, Jade Catta-Preta, Idalis de Leon, Daniela Melgoza
and Jesse Garcia.

FOREWORD

BY LUIS ALBERTO URREA

I don't know if I want to praise Rick Najera or to bury him. We homeboys can be a jealous lot. Every time I see a Najera movie, or see him on cable doing one of his stand-up extravaganzas, I swell with pride and curse him to the depths of my soul. How far you have come, Rick, from our roots. But, as a musician friend once told me: "Roots? There is a whole tree above the ground."

We share some interesting soul-DNA. Both with deep Mexican roots, and both from mixed Anglo/Mexican families. Both from San Diego. Both gueritos—we look like cousins. And both of us were rebel misfit boys who came up through drama and comedy—theater troupes and acting cadres. And both of us, sooner or later, had to flee the sunny confines of home to do battle out there in the bigger world. I feel safe to say that each one of us, in our different disciplines, feels the responsibility to represent. We are both always aware of the other young dreamers lining up behind us, looking for a way to express their art and dreams in the face of overwhelming odds.

You don't have to be Chicano, but it helps.

I know the motives behind this collection are altruistic. No, Najera is no saint. He's as much of a jerk as the next guy. Just listen to his stand-up. You'll join me in saying, "Dude, you can't say that!" Expletives deleted. However, he is deeply aware—having been through the vale on his own journey—how lonely and silent that journey can be. Young actors like us—young "Latino" actors—had precious few words to say that spoke of our experience. There were few bards to give us scenes and one-acts to express that secret soul-space unique and precious inside us. At the same time, the greater culture out there was telling us that our essence was rotten, that we needed to sit down and shut up. Be ashamed, beaner, and mop the floor.

Oh no. No, no. Rick penned these works not only to be good theater— good comedy—big-ass wrestling moves in the heavyweight title match. But he penned these as a kind of profane ministry. Young woman, young man—these words were written for you. These offerings were tossed, like flares, into the dark. For you. My homey wouldn't get this maudlin, but the big dog wrote this with love.

Órale, Najera. Bring it.

—Luis Alberto Urrea

(Luis Alberto Urrea is a Pulitzer Prize finalist and best-selling author of *The Devil's Highway, The Hummingbird's Daughter, Into the Beautiful North, Queen of America* and several other works of fiction, nonfiction and poetry.)

"The audience was in stiches!" - The New York Times

Rick Najera's
LATINOLOGUES

Award-Winning Comedy About Life in America
The Original Collection of Monologues From the Barrio to Broadway & Beyond
Created and Written for Stage by Rick Najera

Plus Bonus Play

BUFORD GOMEZ

Graphics by Momo Rodriguez

LATINOLOGUES™

BY RICK L. NAJERA

BROADWAY SCRIPT

HELEN HAYES THEATER

NEW YORK, NY

OCTOBER 13, 2005

INTRODUCTION

(Lights begin to dim. The on-stage video screen displays Latino-themed spoofs of traditional Broadway play posters such as Cholo Cholo Bang Bang, The Latin King *and* Spanishalot. *Finally, we see the poster for* Mama Mia. *But in our version, the woman is Latina in a frilly, vibrant, colorful dress. A slug line reads: "Support Latinos on Broadway." Then, the screen goes blank. "Boricana's Welcome" plays and the following curtain speech is heard from an announcer off stage.)*

ANNOUNCER: Welcome to *Latinologues*, a comic celebration of Latino life in America. Remember . . . if you must open your 40-ouncer, do it quietly. *Si se van a chingar una Caguama, háganlo en silencio.* Please turn off your cell phones and pagers. *Apaguen sus teléfonos y vibradores.* Remember, photography is strictly prohibited. *No saquen fotos, no estamos* *en el zoológico. Latinologues* is performed in 99 percent English. *¿Cómo que en inglés! ¡No hablo pinche inglés! Because* we don't want the Anglos confused. *Como la confused.* They paid full price, damn it! *Ya me voy a la chingada.* I am outta here!

(SFX: We hear foot steps and a door slam.)

Latinologues is brought to you by Tres Flores y Micky D's. Me encanta high blood pressure and diabetes. Y también La Luna Insurance, when the Virgin on your dash board is your only form of insurance then you better call us.

Ladies and gentlemen . . . *Latinologues.*

ERAZMO

(Lights up. SFX: Loud ranchero music starts blaring. ERAZMO enters doing a mini quebradita *dance, holding a suitcase, hooting and hollering. He wears a large straw hat, jeans and cowboy boots.)*

ERAZMO: *¡Ayyyyyyy ha hayyyyy! Qué viva el mero Norte Sinaloa. ¡Huey! El otro día me estaba chingando una Caguama en la troca con la raza cuando* . . . Oh, you don't know how to speak Spanish? *Pues chíngense porque estamos* en Nueva York, the capital of Puerto Rico. Okay, okay, I have to speak English or they're going to deport me again. My name is Erazmo and I went to the airport the other day to get a cheap plane ticket to Puerto Vallarta because I needed a vacation. I deserved one. The pressures of being head dishwasher at Roxy's Restaurant are huge! So I get to the airport and I see all these immigration guys. INS, DEA, TSA, Triple A, Mary Kay, ATF. ATF—Alcohol, Tobacco and Firearms—sounds like a party I went to in New Jersey. Well, *la migra* was all over the place now. After 9/11, they got an excuse, they're all over the place now and they're looking for terrorists, or dishwashers. A *migra* guy called Buford Gomez threatened to put a baton up my ass and make me look like a candy apple. I get scared. I don't know why, but I get scared. So I did what a good Mexican should do—I run and hide in the bathroom.

Sitting on the toilet where I do my best thinking, I get an idea. Why buy a *pinche* plane ticket to Puerto Vallarta when they can deport me back for free? *¡Ajuua!* So I run up to the immigration guy and say, "Pleeease sir, do not deport me back to that hell-hole Puerto Vallarta, please! I cannot stand one more day lying on the beach with cocoa butter all over my body. No more shrimp tacos for me, nooo. Please do not send me to back to that hell-hole Puerto Vallarta. Or Ixtapa or Cancun . . . . Noooooo!" Next thing you know I'm on a *pinche* Club

Med flight to Puerto Vallarta for free! *¡Me los chingué compa! ¡Ajua!* I even earned 5,000 frequent deportation miles.

Ahhhh, Puerto Vallarta! Life is good in Puerto Vallarta! You can drink your tequila from a coconut, right on the beach. You can eat barbecued fish, right on the beach. You can walk on the beach, with your bitch! I am happy because I am in Mexico. *¡Estoy en mi tierra, compa!* But suddenly, money starts running out. I can't afford to eat at the expensive restaurants that the tourists eat at anymore. Soon I can't afford to eat at the cheap restaurants the Mexicans eat at anymore. I can't afford to eat anymore. So I look to America, and she lures me. She seduces me.

She's like those ladies in the dance halls, you know? Like strip clubs, like Scores.

(To a male in the audience:)

You know Scores? C'mon, I've seen you there! I've passed you coupons in Times Square—Okay, I get it, and you're with the girl.

(Back to general audience:)

Well, those ladies in Scores, from a distance they look beautiful, but up close, *más* Maybelline *que la chingada!*

And before you know it, I'm back at the border . . . and I'm in front of a sign.

(Erazmo turns his suitcase around. The "CAUTION: BORDER CROSSING" sign is painted on it for demonstration.)

That's me, my wife, my kid . . . I know I'm not holding her hand. But she's going to make it, I swear. But look at this sign . . . *(Beat)* It's all wrong! It must have been designed by an American. I mean this family's way too small to be Mexican. There should be at least five more kids. And look! My wife's wearing high heels. *No mames!* You should never wear high heels when crossing highways or deserts. You could die.

This is my natural migration pattern. Mexico to America to work. We are an endangered species here! Fuck the Grey Whale—what about me?

Oh, you know what? I got a present for my friend Alejandro . . . the busboy. *(He pulls out a small rock.)* He's from Colombia, and he's a macho. And sometimes he lets me watcho. I bought him this piece of rock and I told him, "This gift I got you, is part of a pyramid. My people, a thousand years ago, we mapped out the stars. We built great pyramids. We were the sons of the Aztec warriors, a great civilization." And he said, "That's great, Erazmo, but what have your people done lately?"

(Beat) What have my people done lately? What have my people done lately? What have my people done lately, *chingado*? . . . Well, I don't know about my people, but I know what I'm gonna do. I'm gonna run, jump and cross over the border! I mean, I'm joining the Third World Olympics.

(Lights create a strobe effect. We hear a Third World Olympics sports announcer give us a play-by-play. Erazmo mimes along with the announcer's narration.)

THIRD WORLD OLYMPICS ANNOUNCER:

Welcome to the Third World Olympics. Erazmo is a fine competitor. He carbo loads on *chicharrones* and Tabasco, the breakfast of champs. I miss the East Germans, always got the gold in crossing borders. But Erazmo trains by working eighty hours a week with no overtime. Picking tomatoes, picking peaches, picking lettuce, picking his ass. Washing dishes, washing even more dishes. Faster, I said. Move it! He's running and crossing 5,000 miles just to pass out flyers for strip joints in Times Square. And there he goes! Running across a freeway, he's crossed the first lane. What a magnificent runner, like an Aztec God. Like a Cheetah wearing boots. Like a tan blur. Like a light Carl Lewis. He's in the carpool lane. He's almost made it. It's looking good. It's his best time yet. Oh my God! What's that? Where'd that car come from? He's hit! It's over! It's over!

(ERAZMO COLLAPSES AS HE IS HIT BY THE CAR.)

(LIGHTS OUT.)

ERAZMO: *(Painfully, to audience:)*

Somebody call a lawyer. *Dos veintidós veintidós veintidós.*

(LIGHTS OUT.)

René Lavan as Erazmo in Latinologues.

BUFORD GOMEZ

(Pictures of the border are projected on screen. A U.S. Border Patrol Officer, BUFORD GOMEZ with a very heavy Tex-Mex accent walks to center stage as the lights come up. He wears dark sunglasses and holds a stop sign.)

BUFORD GOMEZ *(To audience:)*

Good evening. Welcome to this special seminar on the United States Border Patrol. Allow me to introduce myself, my name is Buford Gomez. I put the panic to the Hispanic. I put the pepper spray to Jose. I put the baton to Juan. Deportation is my business and business is good. I see a strange looking car coming at me and it has an "I heart Puerto Vallarta" sticker on the car. I'll come on up and say, "Hey you with the grandmother that looks like la India Maria, pull it over." "Hey, you there with the eight track of Los Tucanes de Tijuana, pull it over." "I smell *chimichangas* and *chicharrones*, that whole family of eight pull it over." And I'll knock on the trunk of that car—now no Mexican can resist this—you knock on the trunk and say *"¡Qué Viva Mexico!"* "Viva, viva, viva." That works every time. I worked in Arizona but I transferred because they asked me for a birth certificate. I got scared. Arizona is a police state. They are tough. But really, who wants to protect that border there? If you really want to immigrate, go ahead; join the rattlesnakes, roadrunners and red necks.

Now I've been decorated. Mexican-Americans are the most decorated minority there is. I fought in Desert Storm. Desert Storm was hard on us Latinos 'cause first of all every Iraqi looks like a Mexican—swear to God. I swear I saw Bin Laden show up at a *quinceañera* with a 12-pack. I swear I saw Saddam Hussein at a piñata party. My wife came out of the shower with a towel wrapped around her head and I nearly killed her. Don't sneak up on me woman, I'm a vet.

Photo by Alan Mercer

Rick L. Najera as Buford in Buford Gomez.

Now there are a lot of fallacies about Latinos. First of all not every single Latino is Mexican. That's wrong. There are different kinds of Mexicans. There's Puerto Rican-Mexicans. Colombian-Mexicans. Dominican-Mexicans. Any Puerto Ricans here tonight? I love Puerto Rican women. They're always like, "*Ay papi, ay papi.*" I love Puerto Rican women. I had a Puerto Rican girlfriend once. I couldn't get my missile to rise—you know what I'm talking' about? This is way before Viagra—I couldn't get that anaconda into a locked position, you know what I'm saying'? Well she practiced Santeria. Caribbean Latinos practice Santeria. It's different. A Mexican woman will just cook a chicken; a Caribbean woman will sacrifice it. There's a difference. She practiced Santeria and she's got chicken feathers all over the floor . . . chicken heads and she started saying, "*Chango chango babalu day yo day yo.*" Then bam! Like a palm tree I was! The only problem was, I couldn't get it on with her unless she had chicken feathers all over her body. And one night she came home and found me cheating' on her with her down comforter. That's a bad joke. You want to hear a good one? Here's a good Border Patrol joke. "Knock, knock." "Who's there?" "On." "On who?" "On the floor mother fucker, it's the border patrol." I did that joke at the Olive Garden in Times Square and the whole kitchen staff just started running.

You Puerto Ricans are good people but you fry everything. I saw a Puerto Rican fry a salad once. They got a dish called *bacalaito.* Its salted cod, deep fried in batter. It's a fish Krispy Kreme. C'mon now folks. That's a heart attack in a snack. Puerto Ricans point with their mouths. You've seen that? One time I asked a Puerto Rican man for directions and I thought he was coming on to me. Now, Puerto Ricans are legal Mexicans. They are born with citizenship.

Any Cubans here? *(One or two respond.)* One lone Cuban? Seemed like a hundred, didn't it? That's what I love about Cuban people—they exaggerate about everything. They say things like, "*Ay coño,* back in Cuba, I ran the entire petroleum industry, but here in Miami, all I got is a can of gas." "*Ay coño,* back in Havana, my dog was a German Shepherd, and here he's a fucking Chihuahua—that's all I have." If every Cuban had as much land as they say they had in Cuba, Cuba would be a continent, not an island. They've even got Chinese Cubanos. That's true! Isn't that freaky when you see a Chinese man speaking Spanish? "*¡Coño! ¡Ni ha mau, coño!*" That scares the shit out of me. I'm telling you, it's weird. Remember, Cubans are Mexicans with rafts. Let me see, am I forgetting anyone? Dominicans? Dominicans are Mexicans who play baseball really well. I love Dominicans.

What I do is hard. All they give me is a gun and pepper spray. Pepper spray is a spice to a Mexican. It doesn't bother them at all. They're at the border with a quesadilla in one hand flipping me off with the other. It's downright embarrassing. They give pepper spray to their children. "Here you are *cabrón*, have some pepper spray".

Now, we have got all sorts of ways to catch illegal aliens; stings are my favorite. Stings work. I did a sting called "Meet the Baywatch girls and Los Tigres del Norte." I caught so many illegal aliens, I threw back two undersized Guatemalans. Guatemalans are little people. They're like the Leprechauns of Central America. They're like, "Hide the gold! Hide the gold!"

Puerto Ricans are legal Mexicans and Venezuelans are Mexicans with oil. Dominicans are Mexicans who play baseball. Oh yes. Argentineans, you are not European. I repeat: You are not European. Anyone I forget?

(Listens and responds.) Colombians, I don't talk about Colombians. They stay up on coke and coffee figuring out how to kill you. *(Feigning sincerity)* Colombians are real nice.

Now some of you here won some neat prizes tonight. *(He reads names.)* Anyone here with a last name ending with a "Z" or a vowel? *(He awaits the audience response and continues.)* I need you to go to the white van behind the theater now in an orderly fashion because I got you a free trip to Disney World. Oh God, they're rioting. Okay! Alright! I need backup! Oh damn it, it must be the Puerto Ricans leading them on! Okay, I need backup! It's Buford Gomez! Follow me, I'm Buford Gomez!

(SFX: RIOT. LIGHTS CHANGE.)

ALEJANDRO

(Lights up)

ALEJANDRO enters dressed in a tuxedo shirt with black pants and a waiter's apron. On a banner behind him is a picture of a huge can of Bustelo Coffee and other Latin foods. Lights pulse as if we are in a disco or night club.)

ALEJANDRO *(To audience:)*

That's right, baby. I'm a macho. I don't need to apologize for who I am. I'm a real man. I'm a macho. I'm a Latino and Latinos are sexy. I love this party. I'm a macho, but I'm also your busboy.

(Lights change to a restaurant setting. We hear patrons eating dinner and the illusion is broken.)

So if I can get you people anything, just let me know. Tequila, frijol-lays . . . Guacamo-lay . . . me? I take my busboy job very seriously.

(To a female patron)

Pssst, oye mami . . . Psst, oye mamita. You want me baby? You want this Latin lover? You want me? Oh, you want coffee? I'll get it for you. We're a little short-handed tonight. My friend, Erazmo? He's the dishwasher. I think he got deported again to Puerto Vallarta. It's okay. Hey, we're short-handed but that's the only thing that's short around here. Got big hands, big feet, and a big heart.

(To audience:)

Latino men love women. We love to please women, especially blonde women.

(To a blonde in the audience:)

Yes, you. You're a Latin blonde baby—you've got highlights. You're a blonde from the island of L'Oreal.

(To audience:)

Us machos get extra macho points for dating blondes, which can lead to valuable coupons and prizes. A friend I know dated a blonde. He got so many macho points and coupons that he got a barbecue set and World Cup Soccer tickets. There's nothing more macho than a bunch of sweaty, muscular men jumping on top of each other after each goooaaalllllll.

(To a blonde in the audience:)

Ay mami, you're so beautiful and so blonde. You remind me of this blonde woman I used to date. She was beautiful like you. I guess dating is stretching just a bit, but it was a very intense couple of hours.

(To audience:)

I remember meeting her at this fine restaurant. Fine wine. I was looking fine in my tuxedo. Had my name tag on…Alejandrrrro. She was my customer and I was her busboy. We really hit it off. I had been giving her good service for most of the night. The bread was warm and soft but I was hard, working hard. Now she wanted me. "Why me?" I wondered. Was she a food service groupie or maybe she had heard of my legendary rise from dishwasher to busboy in only six short years? Success is an aphrodisiac for women, my friend. Our hands met after I served her some Sweet & Low. It was perfect, she was sweet, I was low. We looked into each other's eyes. She said she lived in Beverly Hills adjacent Encino. I tell her I live in Bel Air adjacent East L.A. She says, "What time do you get off work?" "In five hours, four, three, two, one, fuck it, I quit. Manny, I quit. Jose, cover my shift. Andale *huey*, cover my shift!" I ran after her. I ran after the American dream. I ran after her like the bulls from Pamplona.

I get to her house -- *¡Híjole!* Six bedrooms, seven baths, *un chingón* kitchen . . . Who the hell is this chick? -- And she's all over me, kissing me. It was hot. It was passionate. A bit aggressive. But, for one moment, our inhibitions are gone. We dance the forbidden dance, a naked lambada, a horizontal *quebradita*. The naked Soldier Boy! Each one of us is an ambassador to each other's tribe. Our curiosity is inflamed. Everything is inflamed. I probe her secrets and she probes mine. And she probes, and she probes, and she probes. It wasn't natural, but I liked it! Then she asks . . .

(As the Blonde:)

"Alejandro, is it true Latino men are fantastic lovers?"

(As Alejandro:)

"Yes baby, it's true."

(As the Blonde:)

"Alejandro, is it true Latino men can make love for hours in a row without stopping?"

(As Alejandro:)

"Hours? Well . . . It's true, if it's not tax time or I'm not having immigration trouble. Or I'm not filling out a census form." I was Latino on my form. But I think I'm almost white. That's more my race. I'm less filling with half the pay and all the calories. "Yes baby, it's true."

(As the Blonde:)

"Alejandro, is it true Latino men are hung like bulls?"

(As Alejandro:)

"Okay, who you been talking to? The Cubans? They exaggerate about everything."

(Back to audience:)

Oh, I could marry her and be a part of the American dream, get my citizenship through copulation. I reach for my fiesta colored condom. She slaps it from my hand. Then she hands me her own condoms. She has 24 different brands, a 50-gallon barrel of all natural organic lubricant. Oh, she knows what she's doing. She is shameless. She has a dog collar and leash, but she doesn't own a dog. She's got rubber gloves and I know she ain't a doctor. She's got handcuffs and I know she's no police officer. Ooooo, I start to get scared. I go to run and she grabs me in a headlock. I say, "Hey, be gentle!" What do you mean, "Lick the man in the canoe?" What do you mean, "Paddle faster?" "No, I don't think it tastes like chicken. It tastes more like *bacalaito* . . . Oh, now you did it, now you did it. Say hello to my little friend!"

We begin to make mad, passionate love. Oh, I want her! Oh, I want to invade her. I want to conquer her. I want to possess her!

Rene Lavan as Alejandro.

(Sings West Side's Story's "I Want To Live In America.")

I want to live in America! Okay by me in America!

Oh yeah! Baby, say my name! Alejandro. Roll the rrrrrs, Alejandrrrrrrro. C'mon say my name. Say my name. Say my name.

(Quotes Luke's "It's Your Birthday.")

It's your birthday. It's your birthday. Ugh Ugh Ugh.

(Quotes Juvenile's "Slow Motion".)

I like it like that, she's working that fat. Ugh, ugh, ugh,

(Quotes Daddy Yankee's "Gasolina.")

Dame más gasolina, dame más gasolina . . . . Ugh, ugh, ugh, ugh.

(Screams in orgasmic pain and quotes/sings Young Money's "Bedrock.")

Call me Mr. Flintstone; I can make your bed rock.

(Quotes Pitbull's "Blanco.")

Súbelo no pare dale que esto siga. Súbelo no pare dale que esto siga. Yo abajo y tú arriba. ¡BLANCO! *Acércame tu pantalón.* ¡BLANCO! *Regálame tus* panties. Come on grrr, say my name, Alejandro! Roll the r's. Alejandrrrrrrrooooooooo!!!!!!

25

(He stops suddenly, not wanting to orgasm.)

W, w, w, wait, don't move! Don't move! SSSSSHHHHHHHH!!!!!!

(Mimes giving the woman stimulation. After a moment, he finally orgasms.)

Azucaaaaarrrrrr! Gracias.

The next morning, something marvelous happens. We see the sunrise holding each other like Adam and Eve in the new world. She's not Anglo, she's an angel. I am not a Latin lover, I'm just her lover. I am the one who cherishes and loves her. Yes, love. *¡¡¿Qué?!?* A macho can use the word love. I'm committed to that word. Because, in this lonely world, love does matter. You can sometimes hold it and for a brief second I held her and I held love. I am not Latino or even a man. I am just two dark eyes that she says she loved. Two dark eyes for her to look into, two dark eyes attached to a body, and a soul. I want her to meet my mother and learn to make that mole I love so much. She makes me want to be a better man. She says she'll call me. She'll call me! Well, I don't wait for her. The next day, I call her over and over again. Finally, two weeks later, she returns my call. And she says, "Alejandro, sorry I haven't gotten back to you. I was in Puerto Vallarta. I want you to know that I had a wonderful time. Some of the things you were doing to me were unimaginable. No, no, it was great! Different, but great. But I can't see you anymore." What? Then she says, "I hope this does not add to your feelings of neglect and inadequacies, and abandonment." I don't know what the hell that means. What do you mean I'm just a busboy? Then she's gone. Gone. Sometimes macho wounds and sometimes he is wounded. Hey, don't feel sorry for me. I'm not just some busboy without a name. My name is Alejandro. I'm a macho and as long as I'm a macho, I'll never be just a busboy.

(LIGHTS OUT.)

JOLANDA:
VIRGIN OF THE BRONX

(The on-stage video screen displays shots of a New York City street. Latin hip-hop music blares. Lights go up on a girl with a short skirt and her back to us. She dances the "booty shake," grinding her hips and shaking her body. Finally she turns around to face the audience. This is JOLANDA, and she is very pregnant. Her belly stands out and looks out of place.)

JOLANDA *(To audience:)*

Oh my God. I heard a heartbeat. This baby is beating his drum of life in me. Listen. *(She listens.)* Can you hear that? Listening is important. And y'all better listen up 'cause I got a big, big announcement.

(Happily)

I'm a virgin and this baby is a miracle. *(Angrily)* Don't you fucking doubt me. *(Happily)* I'm a miracle. I'm a virgin. I have not known men. I'm the Virgin of the Bronx. *La Sagrada Virgin del* Bronx. I have had a divine booty call, an immaculate non-contraception, and a Holy pregnancy. God got my digits and I've never known or ever been touched by human men. Okay, I did make out once with some guy in a car after a few Long Island Ice Teas at a Marc Anthony concert on the Jersey Shore, but that's all. For real. I'm not lying. -- I'm the Virgin of the Bronx.

(Sings, like a hymn.)

La Sagrada Virgen del Bronx. I called the *New York Post* to tell them but they said,

27

Photo by Alan Mercer

Monica Ortiz as Jolanda in Jolanda: Virgin of the Bronx.

(As NY Post Rep:)

Lots of virgins in the Bronx got pregnant by men who disappeared.

(As Jolanda:)

But I said, "I was visited by an angel," but they said,

(As NY Post Rep:)

Lots of women got pregnant by guys named Angel, Jesus, Carlos, and Junior.

(As Jolanda:)

They did not believe me. But that's okay, I got a baby now. A real baby right inside me. It's real. Not like that fake Gucci purse I got at Canal Street. I told Ms. Chang that it was not a real Gucci purse and she said,

(As Ms. Chang:)

You get out of my store before I shoot you in the head.

(As Jolanda:)

She had a real anger control problem. Like my mom's, yo. She worked as a waitress and she used to bring me home leftovers and I'd say, "Mami, there's a cigarette butt in my steak." And she'd say,

(As her mom:)

"Malagradecida, desgraciada. ¿Cómo tú me vas a decir esa vaina? Mira ven, cómete esa comida. Sigue ahí que te sueno el fundillo coño."

(As Jolanda:)

That's Dominican for time out. More like knock out. The social worker said my mother had a real anger control problem. She didn't have an anger control problem; she had a "kicking my ass" problem. She was crazy. Sometimes she used to beat me with a clear plastic *chancla*. It was like being beaten by Casper the angry ghost. It was like a stealth slipper. I was like the Latina *Precious*. Oprah, I want a book deal.

But this is my baby. Not some leftover from some plate. Not some fake cheap-ass purse. This baby's a miracle. And I remember the night it happened. I was on my roof at night and it was warm. I heard a voice. It was other worldly.

(As Alejandro:)

Psssst, *oye mami.*

(As Jolanda:)

More like third-worldly.

(As Alejandro:)

Oye, mamita.

(As Jolanda:)

He was an angel that had landed on earth in the form of a busboy named Alejandro. He was like an angel like an appa, appa, Appalachian, or some shit like that. He had a gold chain. I wrote a poem about it and performed it at the Apollo Theater. It goes like this, "Alejandro had a gold chain. Gold, gold, gold like my mother's front teeth. His shirt had yellow stains. Yellow, yellow, yellow, like the freshly fallen snow after the bums in my neighborhood have peed on it. His hair was black and oily like the roof on my apartment building on a hot summer day, day, day. Or like Sammy Sosa." Then I looked into his eyes and said, *"Morenito que está bueno, cualquiera se lo come."* That's Spanish for "Hello." Well then he said,

(As Alejandro:)

"Si cocinas como caminas, guárdame un chin del concón."

(As Jolanda:)

That's Spanish for "Hello to you, too." Then I heard this music from like heaven.

(Heavenly music plays)

That's not my jam!

(Dance hip-hop song plays)

(Jolanda dances)

Then he took my hand like in the *novelas* 'cept I wasn't blonde and speaking Spanish. Then he started dancing real slow. Then we talked on the roof. And he listened to me. His name was Alejandro and it was written on his nametag and tattooed on his chest: Alejandro Francisco Gomez de la Rosa Martin Moreno. And then he took me in his arms and he kissed me and he listened to me. Then we made love. *"Ay mami, ay mami, échale gasolina, ay mami,* call me Mr. Flintstone because I can make your bed rock, *azucar."* Damn, that was fast. It was so beautiful and fast. But it was beautiful for a few minutes . . . seconds. I guess Alejandro had a real control problem, too. Well, it was special. It wasn't long, but it was accurate. Then I got pregnant and then I knew it was a miracle because he just vanished like a vision. Because angels can't stay on earth forever. So don't look at me like I'm a single mother, look at me like I'm a miracle. Because I'm having a baby. Are you listening? Listen, I ain't down, I'm moving like my baby. I'm celebrating my life. *Sí, sí, sí.* Play my jam.

(A Latin hip-hop song plays. She begins to dance as the lights fade out.)

MANIC HISPANIC

(Lights flicker as if in a nightclub. Music plays.)

Our MANIC HISPANIC enters in a whirlwind dancing to techno music. His helper, Paquito enters with him. They dance together as if high on ecstasy or a similar drug. Clearly they're gay.

MANIC: *(To Paquito:)*

Paquito, Paquito, ¡músico más abajo por favor!

(Paquito runs off stage. The music is lowered and finally off.)

(To audience:)

I'm the Latino no one talks about, the Latino professional. And this is my office here in Hollywood. Isn't it beautiful? It's designed by a Hispanic designer and ironically a Hispanic cleans it up at night. And I'm Hispanic. I didn't know I was Latino until this year. I'm like a born again Latino. And once they discovered I was Latino, they put me in charge of the whole *Divisiono de los Latinos del* Paramount Studios. I even adopted a little Latino kid from Bolivia, Fernando. He's the one in the picture with the flies on his forehead. I sent him a few pennies and a postcard and he's so happy. I'm just worried he's going to show up at my house some day and say, "I'm Fernando from Bolivia. You sent me two pennies and one postcard. Fuck you, Daddy." That would hurt. I want to be a good father. Look I brought you in here to give you some good news and bad news.

(Talking to a Latin screenwriter:)

Good news: This market is going to be huge! This is the year of the Latino. And I have to tell you, Mr. Latino screenwriter man, I love your screenplay. "CORTEZ AND MONTEZUMA, FEATHERS OF FURY."

31

Yes. Yes. It's men with shirts off, it's spears, it's Spanish, it's Aztec, it's Spaztec. It's like a party in Chelsea. It was like Ricky Martin's coming out party. What a surprise, I never saw that one coming! That's why the studio gave you this overall deal . . . Well we believe in the Latino market. That's the good news and . . .

Oh my God, we've got so many ideas for *projectos*. You want to see some of our other ideas for *películas* we're developing? OK. This is for the Cubans.

(He refers to a projected slide of the film on a banner behind him as he describes it.

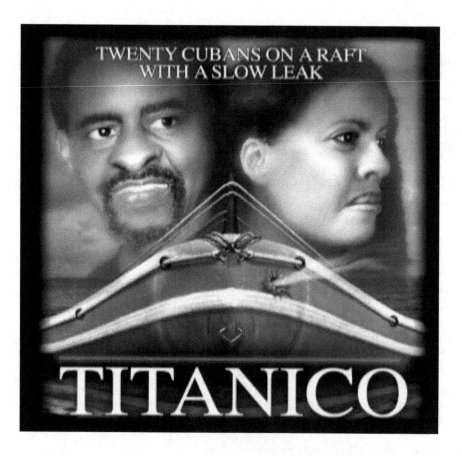

TITANICO: Twenty Cubans on a Raft with a Very Slow Leak. Picture it: "*Coño,* do you hear something? *Coño,* I swear I hear something? Why are the sharks getting so frickin' close, *coño?*"

And for the Puerto Ricans, we've got something historical, a World War II drama . . .

(Next slide.)

Saving Private Martinez. And it goes like this. "Sir, we lost a Martinez at Anzio Beach." "No!" "Sir, we lost a Martinez at Omaha Beach." "No!" "Sir, we lost a Martinez at Jones Beach. There are only 20 Martinez brothers left. We've got to save them." Not very suspenseful, I know.

And for the Dominicans . . .

(Next slide.)

Two hundred pounds of Dominican fun wrapped up in taffeta. Carbo loading on mango, she's going to be huge, I'm telling you. Or another film, a science fiction film about aliens arriving in a piñata from outer space and they try to conquer the world but get jobs as gardeners and maids and just got tired and say: "Screw it. We'll just stay and watch bad Univision shows." District *Nuevo*. And my biggest film idea yet, it's my Latino *Precious.*

(Next slide.)

maria conchita alonso
and introducing
la pumkin garcia

preciosas

Together they made one beautiful
person inside and out

Preciosas! With Maria Conchita Alonso and a little *gordita* from Pacoima. And once we use her we will put her back in the barrio just like those kids in *Slum Dog Millionaire*. And then we'll decide what we'll do with that Maria Conchita Alonso, too. Just leave your keys and computer and the nice security guard will walk you out.

(To audience:)

I'm a 100 percent Latino. I just don't speak Spanish very well. Mea culpa, mea culpa, mea culpa. But that doesn't make me less of a minority. I was on a plane once and a stewardess came up to me and said, "Mr. Martinez, are you Latino?" I said, "Yes, but I'm not leaving first class." Then she said, "There is a man in economy having medical difficulties; we need you to translate using your best Spanish possible." Oh my God, it's *Grey's Anatomy* and I'm McDreamy, here I go. So I run to the back of the plane and there's this man there and he's like, *"Yo soy diabético. Ayúdame."* I don't know what the fuck he's talking about. So I give him some of my Godiva chocolates, I start popping them in his mouth. 'Cause Godiva makes you feel so good. And I'm popping them in his mouth and he's like *"Déjame en paz maricón. Déjame en paz maricón."* And I'm like, "Who the hell is

Marty Cohen, my name is Martinez." So the stewardess is yelling, "Please, Mr. Martinez, translate using your best Spanish possible." So using my best Spanish possible I said, "*Chew are going to die. Muerta. No más aquí. Siga la luz blanco.*"

But I'm 100 percent Latino. I'm Latino and the studio wants to go Latino. And now here's the bad news. They don't want to go with *you*. You are being let go. All those projects are being written by white writers so we won't need you. Sorry, *lo siento*. I tried to find another show for you to be placed on, like George Lopez or Carlos Mencia but they said they don't need Latinos either. What's with our people and helping each other out? There can only be but one. Like in that movie *Highlander*.

I call it the *Hispanic Highlander Syndrome*, there can only be one. There is no nice way to say it, but you are not needed. Why don't you go away and wait 'til we will need you? I wish we could freeze dry you like Luke Skywalker. You'd be frozen until Hollywood needs you again. Then we will just thaw you out.

Oh, I know you know about Cancun. I got that statue in Cancun. I love Cancun and I love Latin artwork. I went there with my roommate Paquito—poor guy. They kicked him out of Menudo when he turned 17. He has shot vocal chords and pelvic arthritis. He just walks around the house singing "*Súbe a mi moto.*" -- They have these great Mayan pyramids in Cancun. And I said to Paquito, "Have you ever been on a Mayan before?" And he said, "Once in Chelsea, long story." So we go, "Let's climb it." *(Beat)* So we walked to the top of this Mayan pyramid. We were like two conquistadors, only with our shirts tied in the middle. And we get to the top of this Mayan pyramid and it was so beautiful and I was truly touched. "*Mi Tierra, con mi raza. Mucho sentimentito aquí.*" So I'm on top of this Mayan pyramid, and I see this little Indian head hidden in the rocks. I was touched. And I said to the little Mayan guy "Ca Ca," which is like Mayan for hello . . . *(Chokes up)* I was touched. I belonged to something. I had a culture, a history. I have no history here in Hollywood. I'm alone and misunderstood, like when I was a *folklórico* dancer and my dad never understood that. Why would I want to dance *folklórico*? Well, you never knew me, daddy. Sorry . . . My inside voice just came out. Well… *(Chokes up again.)*

My Mayan side was in awe, but my Spanish conquistador side thought it would've made a neat bookend. So I broke it off and brought it here to Hollywood.

All right, we've bonded. I feel like I'm with my family only no one is shouting at me in Spanish. Let me show you the dailies from my biggest film yet, it's my Mel Gibson's *Passion*. Roll the tape. . . . No, from the beginning!

(BLACK OUT.)

Photo by Alan Mercer

Rick L. Najera and Chingo Bling in Manic Hispanic.

MEXICAN MOSES

(In the darkness we hear an announcer. The announcer is heard on and off throughout the following scene but he is never seen.)

(ANNOUNCER:) *(Voice over)*

It came about at the time of the cruel Pharaoh, Ronald Reagan. A child was found floating down the Rio Grande River in a Corona beer ice chest. He was found by the daughter of a Republican and raised, not as a Mexican, but as a white child. He did not know he was Mexican, except for a high tolerance for spicy foods and a fascination with Mariachi music. He was the one who would lead the Latino people for he was Mexican Moses.

(Lights reveal a man with huaraches and a small hat on his head holding a staff. He looks like a Mexican version of Charlton Heston from The Ten Commandments.*)*

(MEXICAN MOSES:) *(To George W. Bush:)*

George W. Bush, let my people go free! George W. Bush, let my people go free!

(To audience:)

I am He, Mexican Moses. Once it was discovered that I was Mexican, I was banished into the deserts of Arizona. I spent many a cold night alone, yet I did not touch myself. I didn't, I swear, for I was on a holy mission. I almost died in the deserts but miraculous . . . miraculous . . . *milagrosamente*—I found a catering truck. I was refreshed with a soda and a ham sandwich until the mayonnaise and salmonella hit my stomach, for it had been in the sun. I wandered looking for medical attention. I needed

Kaopectate, adult diapers and a large cork. But I was denied medical attention and a driver's license because they thought I was an illegal alien. It was then that I heard a small, still voice. It was the voice of God.

(A GOD-LIKE VOICE sounding a lot like Cheech Marin is heard. His voice is heard on and off as he speaks to MEXICAN MOSES, but he is never seen.)

(VOICE OF GOD:)

PSST, MEXICAN MOSES! I'M TALKING TO YOU, *VATO!* LEAD THE LATINO PEOPLE FOR I HAVE HEARD THEIR *GRITOS* AND KNOW THEIR TROUBLES. I'VE BEEN WATCHING SPANISH TV, LOOKS BAD. YOU MUST LEAD THEM ON A HOLY JOURNEY TO FIND THE PROMISED LAND, FOR YOU ARE MEXICAN MOSES.

GO TO LOS ANGELES WHERE YOU WILL FIND ALL THE LATINOS AT SWAP MEETS AND FLEA MARKETS. THEN GO TO NEW YORK WHERE YOU WILL FIND ALL THE LATINOS AT THE PUERTO RICAN PRIDE PARADE BUT DON'T DRESS SLUTTY. THOSE GUYS CAN'T KEEP THEIR HANDS TO THEMSELVES. NOW, GET GOING.

(MEXICAN MOSES:) (To audience:)

Latinos? Where are my peeps? Wow, lots of Latinos here. Now the tribe of Cuba to the very, very far right. Now all of those Chicanos to the far left. Puerto Ricans, we leave tonight. Only two chickens per family: One for eating, one for the sacrifice. Dominicans, stop playing baseball and get in line. Listen, I am Mexican Moses. We will learn many commandments like:

(VOICE OF GOD:)

NUMBER ONE: THOU SHALT BE ON TIME.

(MEXICAN MOSES:)

Oh, they'll never do that one. Next.

(VOICE OF GOD:)

NUMBER TWO: THOU SHALT PAY FOR YOUR CABLE TV.

(MEXICAN MOSES:)

Nevermind, everyone's got a cousin with a screwdriver. Next.

(VOICE OF GOD:)

NUMBER THREE: THOU SHALT STOP BOOTLEGGING DVDS.

(MEXICAN MOSES:)

Unless you can get me *Girls Gone Wild.* The desert is a lonely place, Lord, forgive me. I am Mexican Moses so . . . Follow me Latinos!

(ANNOUNCER:) (Voice over)

And thus started the biggest Latino exodus seen since the ending of a Daddy Yankee concert.

(LIGHTS OUT.)

CUBA LIBRE

(Lights up. CUBA LIBRE—an innocent looking, young, attractive Latina walks on stage wearing a faded 50's dress. Her hair is disheveled. She is attempting to look like a 1940's movie actress, but she has faded.)

CUBA LIBRE: *(To audience:)*

"If you want me just whistle. You know how to whistle don't you? You just put your lips together and blow." I've seen that movie 100 million times!

(Coyly)

Oh, I shouldn't say a million. I'm a good communist. *(Fact) Ven aqui, chico.* You have dollars? I bet you got a million.

(Pleading)

Wait. I can see it in your eyes. Don't turn away. Don't think your thoughts. I hear them. They hurt me, they whip me.

(Seriously)

Life is tough here. I sell myself to tourists for dollars to provide for my mother who is suffering from a tropical, malarial, gingivitis disease. Without dollars, you die. There is no more life en Cuba, *chico.* I do what I have to do to survive . . . and I do it very well. Wait, don't go!

(Astonished)

Oh my God, you're unmoved. You must be an American. You have a cold heart. I could warm it.

(Seductively)

I could defrost that cold heart. Warm it within my tropical borders. Save your life, teach you love. I could defrost your heart like a microwave oven . . . cleanly, economically, efficiently.

(She seductively rolls her tongue around her mouth, licking her lips.)

Efficiently. Would you like that?

(Plainly)

I can be a nice girl and sit in your lap. And we can play spin the bottle. "Oh look, you win." And if you're a *marica* boy and you don't like girls, that's okay. We can talk about Judy Garland. But if you do like girls, then prove it chico, rent a room. Oh wait, maybe you have a little *pito* like when you get naked the girls say, "Oh how cute. Two belly buttons." Wait, I could be your tour guide here in Havana. You like Cuban architecture? You like my architecture? My big Latin arches? I have a strongly influenced African culture that is aching for your New England colonial influence to drive me mad with envy and desire.

(Realizing)

You don't like me? I bore you? You don't want me? You led me on you, bastard!

(Angrily)

I gave myself to you. I loved you.

(Weeping)

Go ahead, leave me. Tear out my heart and boil it.

(Threateningly)

Okay, you want trouble? I'll call La Guardia right now and say you tried to rape me. Maybe say you were saying shit about Castro. That you were saying he is an old man with an ugly beard. Oh, he hates that. You don't know what hell is till you spend it in a Cuban jail.

(Angrily, fast)

Coño, ya no se porque yo sigo hablando con este come mierda. Wait, I'm not angry, I'm just Caribbean. All right, a tour.

(Business-like)

This plaza is where Castro plotted with Che right here in this coffee shop. And over there is where my parents met, they sipped coffee. And people stood on those balconies and watched the sunset and applauded the particularly good ones. And they sipped . . . *(Remembering)* Cuba Libre. Here "Cuba Libre" means "free Cuba." Free Cuba, *Cuba Libre.*

(Beat. She drops the act.)

Oh fuck it, rent a room. I'll lie with you for free.

(Slowly)

No dollars, free. I just want to imagine I'm in California with the Hollywood sign behind us and a full moon; and we'll make love in your beautiful home with all the lights on and the windows open. And there will be no shame because I'll be your bride and you'll be my husband. We'll make love not in secret. And I'll lie in your arms. I'll be happy and never dream of Cuba. Rent a room. I'll lie with you for free; at least I'll be off this island. Even for just one moment, even if it's just in my mind. You can have me for free. I can set you free. *Cuba Libre. Cuba Libre.*

(LIGHTS OUT.)

THE WHITE GUY

(Lights up on a "typical white guy." He is in a tuxedo holding a champagne glass in his hand. There is the sound of a wedding crowd underneath.)

WHITE GUY: *(To audience:)*

I love Maria, okay? That's the first thing you need to know about us. There is love here. Not *telenovela* love that I see on her mother's TV set. Boy, they sure talk fast, don't they? Wow, it's like, slow down Maria. I lost you around somewhere between when you opened your mouth and you closed it, which in a Latina's case is never. Come on, I'm kidding. *Es un chiste.* I'm kidding. You Latino guys are nodding your heads. I see you. No, come on, *es un chiste.* Come on.

Marriage doesn't come with a manual. I had to learn that quickly. When my wife Maria yells at me in Spanish, it's like she can tell me what is wrong with me and all our issues and what bothers her about me, in two minutes of Spanish. That would take an Anglo woman in English at least two years of talking and six months of group therapy. I don't speak Spanish as you all know. And I'm not stupid but the words I hear, I swear, they don't teach you those at Berlitz. You never hear what I hear at a Berlitz course. Unless it's Puerto Rican Swear Words 101 and I know you all like to kid me about me not speaking Spanish. *Yo no soy* stupid okay? I hear you talk.

(Points, as Tío Alfredo:)

Greg, your little nephew Paco is only two and he speaks better Spanish than you.

(As himself:) Funny, Tío Alfredo, very funny. But Paco, he has nothing to do but eat, crap, piss and learn Spanish all day. OK. But call me ANGLOSARUS REX. I admit it, I'm a dinosaur.

(To audience:)

I respect Latin women; I married one. I give her respect. It's very important in Latin culture. I learned that sometimes her family didn't feel I was respecting them. And they'd get mad for like . . . forever. Because Latinos got a thing called "Latino Alzheimer's." They forget everything but a grudge. Latinos love fantasy. Us Anglos like facts and figures and science. There are differences between our cultures. You'll learn this once you get married. Oh, and I didn't marry her because of some strange white guy guilt or some strange white guy sexual fascination for Latinas, but she is good in bed. I mean great, but there are white women just as good in bed, but with them you don't have to marry them. They don't want to get married. They're sluts according to my wife. And I'm glad I married into this family. Mamá, Papá, *te amo.* They came to the wedding with her family meeting mine. My family is from New England and they were shocked. And they are very white, translucent white.

(To his wife:)

Lots of laughs there, hey baby?

(To audience:)

My family's from the island of Nantucket. Her family's from the island of Puerto Rico. Her family—nice, tropical, warm people. And mine are witch burning, whale killing, and fun-loving New England people. Clam bakes and witch burning, we love to cook and entertain. Her family—from Puerto Rico, loud and large. They love kids or sex; I don't know which one they love more. We had 2.5 kids in my family. We lived in clapboard old New England houses. Her family lived in a nice house. Not a grass hut according to my Uncle Ben. That's so ignorant. Puerto Ricans live in palm huts. Everyone knows that. -- I'm kidding. It was a nice house unless it was hurricane season; then they lived in a nice shelter.

Hurricanes are big in Puerto Rico. It seems that they remember everything by hurricanes or when some one lost their job.

(Latino accent, as a Puerto Rican:)

Remember last Christmas when Freddie lost his job or two years ago during hurricane Yolanda?

(To audience, as himself:)

Oh, my wife found an interesting historical fact. Interesting historical fact.

You know in New England, those clapboard houses were named after the clap that New England whalers brought home with them? That's what Maria told me. There are cultural differences that you will find such as language. English is a scientifically precise language. Spanish is a beautiful language, a romance language, which means you'll get laid but you won't build a rocket ship.

I didn't marry my wife because I thought it was cool or I was a white guy that wanted to be "down with brown." Or I loved the food so much I had to marry a cook. I do love the food. I do. They got a food called a *bacalaito*—its salted dried cod fish, fried in bread. It's a fish donut.

Or I wanted to be cool like those white guys that get possessed by a black man every time they speak hip-hop. I married my wife, Maria, because of an accident. I didn't plan it. I just fell in love. It was an accident like the invention of the phone or discovering America, it was an accident. I think we've had a good time, Maria and I. Our marriage has not been quiet or easy, it's been better than that. It's been loud, passionate, sexy, rhythmic and fun.

(He dances a little salsa move.)

She taught me that. I taught her the chicken dance.

I remember a story I once heard and it goes like this . . . Adam and Eve once had many children and their children traveled for many generations in different directions. One day they ran into each other in a great old forest in the middle of the world. And at first they only heard each other coming. They could not see each other. They only heard each other. So they grew very frightened, because all people get scared of what they don't know or understand. So they beat their shields together to scare off the other tribes. *(Beat)* And they beat their shields together. *(Beat)* And they made a great noise to scare their imagined enemies, but this only scared the other tribes more. Finally they threw their spears and filled the sky with spears and arrows and there was a horrible slaughter before they all figured out they were once brothers and sisters.

I think in the end, we all are family. And sometimes we have to remember that. And marriage reminds us of that. I hope you always remember that in your marriage. So Carlos, you are my brother-in-law and best friend, and Shoshanna you are my co-worker and the best CPA partner in the tri-state area. I wish you both all the happiness in the world together and hope you find the love I found by accident.

(LIGHTS OUT.)

JUAN MIGUEL GONZALEZ

(Lights change. We hear tropical music. Pictures of Miami rafters and news clips of Elian Gonzalez are projected on the on-stage video screen. An actor enters holding a phone and wearing a Che Guevara T-shirt. It's JUAN MIGUEL GONZALEZ, Elian Gonzalez' father. He wears shorts.)

JUAN MIGUEL GONZALEZ: (Into phone:) Hello? Hello, Castro? Fidel? Fidel Castro?

(To audience:) Coño, I got through.

(Into phone:) Is this *El Grande Comandante,* Fidel Castro? Hi Fidel. This is Juan Miguel Gonzalez, Elian Gonzalez' father. *Coño* Fidel, how could you not remember Elian? You know the little Cuban kid who nearly drowned off the coast of Miami. Elian: E-, L-, I-, *(Tries to spell) La fea* took back my kid. No, not Betty La Fea. The real *la fea,* Janet Reno. She took back my kid! *(ELIAN is heard off stage. His voice is that of an overgrown child.)*

ELIAN: Papá, Papá.

JUAN MIGUEL GONZALEZ: (To Elian:) Shhh Elian.

(Into phone:) No, he's okay. He's only going through puberty right now. Yes. Actually, Fidelito we were just calling to say hello. You know, it's been about five years now and I noticed no one is paying much attention to me and Elian. Now, Fidel you promised if I came back to Cuba you would give me things. You know a job and toys for the boy— at least soap and toilet paper. Yes, yes I did get the presents you sent for the boy. But Fidel, they were just a little cheap. Yeah. Cheap. Come on, Fidel . . . *(He holds up a sponge.)* This is not Sponge Bob. It's a fucking sponge. Yes, we got the Golden Retriever puppy you sent us. I named

him Lechón. He's not a Golden Retriever, he's a pig. That's why I named him Lechón.

ELIAN: *(OFF STAGE)* I love Lechón.

(ELIAN enters wearing "Water Wings" and swim trunks. He is huge and overweight.)

ELIAN: I love my puppy, Lechón!

JUAN MIGUEL GONZALEZ: *(To Elian:)* Elian, don't get too attached to that pig because he's going to be golden soon enough.

ELIAN: I want to go back to Miami, Cuba sucks.

JUAN MIGUEL GONZALEZ: *(Into phone:)* No, no he's just got a little thyroid problem or something. I think they fed him too much chicken in Miami. He's growing too fast. By the way, this is not a Slip 'n Slide, Fidel. *Coño*, a plastic sheet on the ground is not a Slip 'n Slide.

(ELIAN attempts to slide on the plastic.)

ELIAN: *Mis huevos, coño.*

JUAN MIGUEL GONZALEZ: *(Into phone:)* Sure, I read the instructions. "Magical Slip 'n Slide. Just add water and imagination." But that's the problem: he doesn't like the water, Fidel.

ELIAN: *(SCREAMING)* NO WATER, NO WATER! I want to go back to Miami. Cuba sucks.

(ELIAN exits quickly.)

JUAN MIGUEL GONZALEZ: *(Into phone:)* The boy is right, Fidel. Back in Miami we had Disney's Magic Kingdom. All we have here is Castro's tragic kingdom.

ELIAN: *(Off stage)* Mickey Mouse. I love Mickey Mouse. I love Mickey Mouse. I want to play with Mickey.

JUAN MIGUEL GONZALEZ: *(To Elian:)* Come here. Come here. I want to talk to you. It's okay. It's okay.

(ELIAN enters) You see that rat over there? Go ahead and play with that rat. He's like Mickey Mouse, but meaner and stronger. Use your imagination.

(Into phone:) Yes, well no Fidel. Actually I am complaining. You promised me things. You promised me a home, some toilet paper and even a toilet. I want to travel to the United States and when I do, I want to be younger than the Buena Vista Social Club. I want some freedom. I want some rights. I want some attention. Right now!

(Suddenly we hear cars driving and helicopters. It sounds like a military assault. Then we hear banging on a door.)

ELIAN: *Soldados. Soldados.* Papá, Papá, Papá, Papá . . . Run, Papá. Run, Lechón.

JUAN MIGUEL GONZALEZ: *(Into phone:)* Oh, that was quick, Fidelito. You're faster than Bush getting to a hurricane. I was only kidding. You've been punked!

(Running off, to audience:) Free education. Free me. Run Elian, run!

(FADE OUT.)

Rick L. Najera and Eugenio Derbez in Juan Miguel Gonzalez.

49

MAMA

(Lights up on a "woman" dressed in black, sitting in a chair. She looks like a typical grieving widow; her white hair is under a church shawl.)

MAMA: *(To audience singing:)*

La Guadalupana, la Guadalupana, la Guadalupana bajo al Tepeyac...

(She stops.)

Thank you so much for being here tonight, I really appreciate it. Sorry about the lights, but they bother my Jose.

(To Jose off stage:)

Jose, wake up! We have visitors. *Visita.*

(To audience:)

Ay, my Jose is a good boy. He's so strong, so macho. I raised him well. All my boys are good boys, even Alfredo. His wife called me and told me he beat her. And I said to her, *"Pues,* what did you do?" He would never do that because he's a good boy.

(To Jose off stage:)

Jose, wake up! There's no light. I shuttered the windows and made you *menudo.*

(To audience:)

No! It's not a hangover. Don't you think that. *Ay,* I worry about my Jose. All the crime in this neighborhood, random violence, gangs. I miss El Salvador. There is no random violence in El Salvador. In El Salvador, the death squads came to your house, took you away, you were dead. Professionals. Here, the violence is random. I worry about Jose because I spoil him. But all Latina mothers spoil their children. Like Dolores. You know Dolores. Dolores Conchita Ramirez Mama Chocha de La Berga Jones. She spoils her boy, the "professional bike rider" like she says. Ha! C'mon Dolores, he's not Lance Armstrong. He has to wear that bike helmet because he's a HEADBANGER! And I heard that is not the only head he bangs! But you know you have to love your children even if they were born stupid.

(To a specific male in the audience:)

Verdad, mijo?

(Back to general audience:)

For example, I have one fine son, Buford. He's a Border Patrol Agent. And he can never get fired. He's like someone who works for the postal service, but less violent. But his younger brother Jose, my gangster son, is not doing so good. I had him later in life, my eggs were bad. They had expired. Even though I love him so much!

Photo by Alan Mercer

Eugenio Derbez as Mama in Latinologues *on Broadway.*

(To Jose off stage:)

Jose! ¡*Ya levántase huevón!* There's no light. I covered the windows.

(Back to audience:)

No! It's not a hangover. It's worse. The truth is, that my Jose . . . is a vampire. *Un pinche* vampire. He's one of the un-dead. At least he's not one of the undocumented. That would be worse. ¡*Pinches indocumentados!*

I still remember the first day I saw the strange marks on his neck. I said, "Have you been seeing that *puta La Chochicaliente*?" He said, "No!" That was when I noticed his hatred of crosses. You can imagine my embarrassment. We being Catholic and all . . . And me, the head of the Daughters of the Inquisition committee and church legal defense fund! Then I started finding blood everywhere. I found bottles that said "Bloody Mary." Poor girl. Then I started finding dark clothing, and white face makeup and eyeliner. That's when I said, "*Mijo*, we should talk." That's when he told me, "Mama, I'm a vampire!" "A vampire!! Thank God, I thought you were gay!" I said.

Like Maria's boy, the one who danced *ballet folklórico* and became a big Hollywood producer. I saw his movie *Mexican Moses*. It flopped! But the actor was gorgeous!

Oh, my poor Jose. A vampire. You should hear him at night, wailing and screaming. At first, I thought it was the Puerto Ricans next door. I hear them at night. "*Ay papi; Ay mami.*" I was going to call social services. *Desgraciados.* Sometimes doing the nasty, not for procreation, but for pleasure!

(To a specific female in the audience:)

Don't laugh, young lady, don't laugh. You must be one of the Puerto Ricans. Listen, I never did it for pleasure. It was two minutes of duty. Stop looking.

(Back to general audience:)

But . . . Well, I just have to remain positive. A vampire is not that bad. At least he's not like Lupita's boy, the werewolf. Her son thinks he's a werewolf. The boy was bitten by Maria's Chihuahua. So every full moon he grows hair all over his body, pees on carpets and bites the neighbors. He bit me. I still have the scar. Look!

(She shows the audience her butt.)

By the way, the Neighborhood Watch has been complaining. They want to throw us out of the neighborhood. Ay, those people. They are not so high and mighty. The other night I saw Mr. Rodriguez watching me during my shower. *Cerdo. Enfermo.* Strike him dead, Lord! Strike him dead! Thank you, Jesus!

(SFX: Growling)

(To Jose off stage:)

No Jose! Get back! Back you child of darkness!

(Praying on her knees.) "*Bendito, bendito, bendito es el Señor!*"

(Back to Jose:)

The power of Christ compels you! The power of Christ compels you, fucking freak!

(She walks off stage. Lights slowly dim.)

THE JANITOR

(In the darkness we hear a man whistling a tune. He is dressed as a Dominican janitor. Behind him, he wheels in a janitor dolly filled with cleaning supplies.)

CARLOS: *(To audience:)*

Sorry. I'm not important. I clean here, that's what I do here. You make a mess and I'll clean it, but I clean real good you know? I clean real good. When I was a kid in Dominican Republic, people would say, "Hey, Carlos what are you going to do when you grow up?" "Oh, I'm going to clean things, 'cause I clean very good." Besides, I was the only Dominican kid that couldn't play baseball; I had to clean. But I was always ambitious. I always wanted to come to the United States of America and be a janitor. At least I found my occupation. I clean—that's what I do. I clean very good. I clean very, very good. People they say to me, "Carlos you're in America now, in America we use chemicals. Chemicals, chemicals, chemicals." Okay! I got a cart full of chemicals, but sometimes the natural stuff works the best.

(To a specific person in the audience:)

Oh man, you look like you like to drink your tequila every once in a while. You mix it, you throw up . . . nothing cleans up vomit better than sawdust, and if it's cedar sawdust, even better. Write it down. That's a trade secret I just gave you. Sawdust for vomit, okay?

(Back to general audience:)

When I first came to America, I had a good job. I got a job as an elementary school janitor. That was a good job. I used a lot of sawdust there. Flu season or chili day? I saw some bad things; I don't like to talk

54

about that. This one kid he threw up so bad . . . the wall was like a mural. It was like the Sistine Chapel but with Captain Crunch and Fruit Loops. *Ay carajo.* I got a promotion after that. They made me high school janitor. Ay, that was a good job. High school janitor. They actually gave me a master key to all the kids' lockers and when they were in class I would go in and steal their marijuana. You smoke one of those marijuana cigarettes and those fish tacos from the cafeteria taste gourmet. High school janitor; that was a good job, man!

I had to get out of high school; too much violence in high school. That Columbine thing scared the crap out of me man. When white kids go bad, they plan it. 9 a.m.: kill classmates. 9:10 a.m.: kill teachers. 10:20 a.m.: kill myself. *Ay carajo.* That won't happen in a Latino school. I guarantee that won't happen in Latino school. 'Cause they'll never get there at the same time. One will show up at 9, one at 3, one at 5... One won't show up and have a really good excuse the next day why he missed the shootout.

. . . I got out of high school. After that I got my dream job. I got my dream job in the city; I work in one of those big office buildings. Easy work. Easy. All I had to do was clean 20 floors at night and 20 floors during the day; I made a lot of overtime there. *Mucho guardo. Mucho dinero.* I even met a girl. She worked at the restaurant upstairs; I worked downstairs. We would meet half way.

Photo by Alan Mercer

Rene Lavan as the janitor in The Janitor.

I like living in the city and working in the city. 'Cause I would see all kinds of things. I'd walk in on bosses having sex with their secretaries and sometimes just having sex by themselves . . . ¡Sinverguenzas!

Oh, the girl I was telling you about? She was from Honduras. I fell in love with her and I wanted to marry her and I did. I was so happy because if you can make it as a janitor in NYC, you can make it anywhere. *(Beat.)* I remember those buildings.

(Lights go up on stage. Reveal two simple beams of light against the wall resembling the Twin Towers.)

I was cleaning up that morning when the first plane hit. Ay, what a mess. There was smoke and dust everywhere. Then the second plane hit. Then they fell. My big beautiful buildings fell to the ground. I lost a lot of friends there: other janitors, busboys, and dishwashers from the restaurant upstairs. A lot of Latinos. But you're not going to hear about them on the reports. They were not reported because they were illegal aliens. Why do people have to make messes that they can never clean up? I stayed and helped with the clean up and a big man comes to me and says, "Why are you here? You're not a fireman." And I said, "I clean, sir. That's what I do. I clean. And I'm going to be here until there's nothing left to clean up. Or until I find my wife."

(BLACKOUT.)

THE PHARMACIST'S MONOLOGUE: PART 1

(The lights go dim. We hear Tijuana Norteño music. On the projector on the back stage wall is a WANTED poster for BENNY "EL FLACO" —a drug lord that has been found at the border. He's from Tijuana. The poster reads, "Reward: $2 Million Dollars." Our actor BENNY'S face is plastered across the poster.)

BENNY: *(To audience:)* They call me a drug lord.

BODYGUARD: He's a drug lord.

BENNY: I'm a drug lord.

BODYGUARD: Drug lord.

BENNY: I admit it, I'm a drug lord.

BODYGUARD: He's a drug lord.

BENNY: But I'm a good man.

BODYGUARD: He's a good man.

BENNY: I'm a good man

BODYGUARD: He's a good man.

BENNY: I'm a fucking good man

BODYGUARD: 'S a fucking good man.

BENNY: I did kill that bishop one time, but that was a mistake.

BODYGUARD: A mistake.

BENNY: A mistake.

BODYGUARD: A mistake.

BENNY: It wasn't me; it was the men who work for me. It's ironic.

BODYGUARD: Ironic.

BENNY: Professional killers can't seem to kill the right person. Gang bangers never kill the other gang bangers. They kill the old woman or the guy with the full scholarship to Princeton. And the other gang—banger is wearing a red and gold jacket. He's kicking it.

BODYGUARD: Kicking it.

BENNY: Kicking it.

BODYGUARD: Kicking it.

BENNY: I have a cocaine problem.

BODYGUARD: YES!

BENNY: I don't have a problem getting it here. I can get as much free cocaine as I want.

(Pulls out a brick of cocaine.)

I like the way it smells.

(Snorts cocaine.)

But it just keeps me up at night. I been up for two years.

BODYGUARD: He's been up for two years.

BENNY: I have a beautiful wife.

BODYGUARD: Beautiful.

BENNY: Beautiful wife.

BODYGUARD: Beautiful. Everyone wants to make love to my wife.

BENNY: Everyone wants to fuck his wife.

BODYGUARD: She's an ex-*telenovela* star. I saw her on the TV and I bought her. Home Shopping Network. Do you want to see a scene from a *telenovela*?

BODYGUARD *(Yelling at audience)*: Answer!

BENNY *(To his wife off stage)*: *Mujer! Vieja,* come and show my guests here a scene from your *telenovela.*

(Benny's wife THALIA walks on stage.)

THALIA: *Son las cuatro de la mañana. Ayúdame.*

BENNY: Do the scene, baby. The scene.

(THALIA prepares to do the scene. Benny's bodyguard joins her. They briefly do vocal exercises and stretch.)

THALIA & BODYGUARD *(Together)*: Scene.

(THALIA and Benny's bodyguard perform an overly dramatized love scene straight from a Spanish language television soap opera.)

THALIA: *Enrique, es tu hijo.*

BODYGUARD: *No, María. No es me hijo.*

THALIA: *Sí, es tu hijo.*

BODYGUARD: *No, no es me hijo.*

THALIA: *Maldito, sí es.*

BODYGUARD: *NO.*

THALIA: *SÍ.*

BODYGUARD: *NO.*

THALIA: *SÍ.*

(She slaps him. He slaps her back.)

THALIA & BODYGUARD *(Together)*: NO!

BENNY: No! See that's acting. It's ironic. I'm the most powerful man in my country but I sit here in my house that I can never leave and I just think. I see ironies all around me. So I'm watching CNN 'cause I can't sleep and I hear about Juan Garza, a convicted drug king pin, that was executed in the State of Texas by lethal injection. Ironic, no? And for his last meal he ordered . . . a steak, French fries and a Diet Coke.

BODYGUARD: A *Diet* Coke?

BENNY: A Diet fucking Coke. Now, I really can't sleep because I'm thinking, "Why would anyone have a Diet Coke?"

BODYGUARD: A Diet Coke.

BENNY: Are you really that worried about the extra calories? Your last meal should be as fattening and as bad for you as possible. For my last meal, I want French fries smothered in some Ebola virus, green monkey piss, and ketchup, salted and sprinkled with some West Nile virus. I want my last meal served to me by a leper with SARS. I don't want U.S.D.A. approved meat. I want a big hunk of mad cow disease meat and I want it served raw. I want my last meal while I'm bungee jumping off the Empire State Building with a dirty heroin needle in one ass cheek, and a dirty cocaine needle in my other ass cheek, and a lit stick of dynamite stuck up my ass while I'm screwing a prostitute with no condom on. And when I come—KABOOM!

BENNY & BODYGUARD *(Together)*: Now that's a real fucking last meal.

(LIGHTS GO BLACK.)

Curtain call for The Pharmacist's Monologue (l.–r.): Marcus Ray, Jose Yenque, Rick L. Najera and Camille Guaty.

MISS PUERTO RICAN DAY PRIDE PARADE

(Graphics of beauty images, quinceañeras *and beauty shops are projected. Oldies music mixed with rap music plays. Then, music with a glamorous sweeping sound is heard. Music stops. Audience and stage go dark.)*

(VOICE OVER:)

Ladies and gentlemen, please give applause of appreciation to Miss Puerto Rican Day Pride Parade as she takes her final walk before she gives up her crown to one of these lucky girls. The Miss Puerto Rican Day Parade is sponsored by JC Penney, Papo's Cuchifritos and Café Bustelo. Café Bustelo—fueling Caribbean angst for over a hundred years. And now we present to you Miss Puerto Rican Day Pride Parade.

(Lights up to reveal MISS PUERTO RICAN DAY PRIDE PARADE walking to center stage.)

MISS PUERTO RICAN DAY PRIDE PARADE:

(Stops center stage and waves. To audience/crowd:)

I have so many wonderful memories of my reign as Miss Puerto Rican Day Pride Parade. The many *quinceañeras* I attended to give those little girls and their fathers hope. 'Dito, after spending as much on their little girls' sweet 15 as on their mortgage. Glamour was worth it, ¿*verdad*? Maybe one day, she would grow up to be Miss Puerto Rican Day Parade. That's if she'd stop feastin' on the *alcapurrias*, the *lechón*, the *pasteles*, and took beauty makeup lessons at JC Penney like I did.

I want to thank JC Penney, who sponsored me for this event. *Coño,* thank you. Also, I want to thank your regional manager, Burt Williams. Oh shit, Burt's in the house. What's good, son? Is that your wife? The one you said didn't understand you? Bitch. Burt Williams said when it comes to contests and pretty young girls, I was the contestant he most wanted to enter. He loved entering me (in contests) whenever he could. So many wonderful memories. I have been honor-ed-ed to lead my peeps as Miss Puerto Rican Day Pride Parade. I am so happy.

(Sings to the tune of "Evita.")

"Don't cry for me, Puerto Rico. I will never forget you. Not in my wild days at the Copa, which were only "rumors" spread by Chata Gonzales' mother, who tried to get me killed so her little fat girl could win my crown. Yeah, that's you bitch. I know where you live. Now, I must give up my crown to one of these contestants. I must turn over my power, after only one short year?

(Pulls out gun.)

Nigga, please! Did y'all think I was going to give up my crown this easily? Huh? Huh? Huh? Give up my scholarship to ITT Tech, where I could learn an exciting career as a nurse's assistant, or a nuclear scientist in six weeks or less? Give it all up after I gave it all up. No fucking chance, ¡sánganos!

(To guards off stage:)

Guards, lock the doors.

(To general audience:)

The military is in control now. What, what! I have exposed the plot to force me to give up my crown and I am not going to give it up to one of these no-talent having, baton-twirling wannabe bitches from old San Juan!

(To a beauty contestant in the audience:)

I know you been blowing out your hair, show your roots *sucias*.

(To general audience:)

What? I've worked too hard. All those lunches with sleazy politicians. I lipo-sucked and plucked my body into this unnatural shape. I got rid of two ribs y'all. I got less bones than a jelly fish. All for men. Alright nobody move!!! My princesses will form a junta with me as their military leader and ruler, along with the help of my multi-national corporation, JC Penney, and the CIA—The Chismosa Intelligence Agency—and my American advisor, Burt Williams.

(To Burt Williams:)

Yeah, papi—you my bitch now. *Te jodiste cabrón.*

(To general audience:)

I want the editor of *Bling Bling Magazine* who took the unflattering pictures of me in a one-piece bathing suit when I had some water retention and my *panza* was sticking out, I want him to be taken out and shot. And people . . . nobody needs to get hurt. Did y'all really think I was gonna give up my crown this easily? Yeah right!

(Hisses as if possessed.)

But please don't worry. My reign will be glamorous and beautiful . . . Unless the people don't obey me. Don't fuck with Miss Puerto Rican Day Pride Parade! I promise free liposuction for the fat ones, free purple eye shadow for my Mexican Cholas, spandex bike pants for the Dominicans, big hoop earrings for my Boricua home girls, and Weight Watchers, reduced calorie *tostones* for everyone. *Wepa!!!!*

Photo by Alan Mercer

(Miss Puerto Rican Day Pride Parade trails off as we hear the Evita *music swell. BLACK OUT.)*

Shirley A. Rumierk as Miss Puerto Rican in Miss Puerto Rican Day Pride Parade.

Erazmo Rest in Paz

(We hear funeral music. Lights go up. ALEJANDRO enters. It's a funeral parlor. The shadow of a casket is on the floor in front of them.)

ALEJANDRO *(He speaks to his dead friend Erazmo):* Oh Erazmo, you were my friend. I loved you. I brought you your favorite beer. *(Opens a beer.)* I must drink it for you. They found your wallet. They found it in your Donna Karens. God, you loved those jeans. *(Opens his wallet.)* Oh there's a picture of his girlfriend! Damn. I must comfort your girlfriend and spend your money.

(Searches through his wallet.)

(To audience:)

He owed me 20. *(Takes money.)*

(To Erazmo:)

Erazmo, men like us are few and far between. And when we meet, we must kill each other.

(To audience:)

Erazmo was a macho and a hell of a dishwasher. All he wanted to do was cross the border and come to America to look for a job. Oh, Erazmo.

(MAMA GOMEZ, the same actor who played the older woman with the vampire son, and BUFORD GOMEZ walk out onto the stage and join Alejandro.)

Photo by Alan Mercer

René Lavan as Erazmo in Erazmo Rest in Paz.

MAMA GOMEZ: No, Erazmo! Nooooooo. Erazmo! Oh, Buford. He was a good man even though he was a pinche illegal. Why Lord? Why Lord?

BUFORD: Because America needs cheap labor.

MAMA GOMEZ: I self-medicated myself with tequila. I better keep self medicating myself.

BUFORD: I thought that was holy water.

MAMA GOMEZ: It is to me.

BUFORD: Maybe a border is something we should share not something that separates us.

MAMA GOMEZ: Erazmo was a big man.

BUFORD: He seemed short to me but that is a closed casket.

MAMA GOMEZ: No, a big man. I have a confession to make. I was a sex worker in Puerto Vallarta and Erazmo was my lover. I worked in the Bar Adelitas de Puerto Vallarta.

BUFORD: Mama, you mean you were a hostess?

MAMA GOMEZ: NO, I MEAN A HO!

BUFORD: You just had to sell drinks mama and be a hostess. You mean you were a hostess.

MAMA GOMEZ: Sure, you can be a hostess but the real money is in screwing the guys. So I did.

BUFORD: What?

MAMA GOMEZ: C'mon, grow up! It was just sex. I screwed less guys than those *putas* on MTV spring break. Erazmo was fucked up by that car.

BUFORD GOMEZ: Mama, your mouth!

MAMA GOMEZ: I'm sorry. I don't mean to have a filthy mouth. But it was appropriate. In the old days, no one cursed unless it was appropriate. Like in Custer's last stand. Custer used bad words. He said, "Holy shit! Look at all the fucking Indians." Because it was appropriate. A border could not hold him and neither could a condom.

BUFORD GOMEZ: Mama, what the fuck are you saying!

ALEJANDRO: No cursing!

MAMA GOMEZ: No, it's appropriate. Buford, I have another confession. Erazmo was your father.

ALEJANDRO: Wow, Erazmo really was a macho!

MAMA GOMEZ: Buford, you were born in Mexico. We crossed illegally when you were only one year old because you could still fit in the glove compartment of our coyote's car. If you look at your head it says GENERAL MOTORS. You are a WET BACK. And I am a *PUTA*!

BUFORD GOMEZ: Mama, don't ever say that. Don't ever call me a wetback.

(*A priest's voice is heard from off stage. It sounds very much like Cheech Marin.*)

PRIEST: Would the family of the deceased like to speak, perhaps his son?

René Lavan as Alejandro in Erazmo Rest in Paz.

Photo by Alan Mercer

BUFORD GOMEZ: That hasn't been proven yet. It was bad what happened to Erazmo. I found him lying on the side of the road; he was wearing cowboy boots and jeans. He looked like a cowboy and he looked a lot like me.

MAMA GOMEZ: I told you. I was a *puta.*

(She drinks.)

BUFORD GOMEZ: Mama, stop drinking!!!! MAYBE YOU AINT' CRAZY AND MY BROTHER IS A VAMPIRE. What I mean to say is Erazmo was trying to come to this country to work. But what doesn't work are borders. The Great Wall of China didn't work. The Berlin Wall didn't work. Hadrian's Wall didn't work. Hell Erazmo's condom didn't work.

(JOLANDA enters.)

JOLANDA: Flower delivery for Erazmo.

MAMA: Ay! Erazmo!

ALEJANDRO: Jolanda?

JOLANDA: Alejandro?

ALEJANDRO: I been looking for you.

JOLANDA: I've been looking for you too. I'm pregnant.

ALEJANDRO: I'm fucked.

MAMA GOMEZ & BUFORD (*Together*): No cursing.

ALEJANDRO: It was appropriate! We're having a baby!

JOLANDA: A baby girl!

ALEXANDRO: But I'm a macho.

JOLANDA: And I'm a virgin.

BUFORD GOMEZ: I'm a WET BACK.

MAMA GOMEZ: I'm a *PUTA*.

BUFORD GOMEZ: Ok, come on people knock it off. Look we came to honor a man that gets no honor. Maybe I have learned something from this tragedy. Look, there are over 45 million Latinos in the United States. Erazmo was one of those people. His was a tragic story but a story nonetheless. We came here to honor him. Look at us. We are hard to describe and nobody seems able to get us. But you know us and we knew Erazmo. He's one of us and his life taught me that. It's not what he was, it was who he was. And he was a good hard-working man that was not documented. Just a piece of paper separated him from us. But us remembering him, well that documents or validates his life. He was like all of us he was many things

(*Slides come up with various pictures of the cast of characters from the show*)

He was and we are your friends, your teachers, your busboys . . .

(*Light on ALEJANDRO.*)

Your neighbors, your lovers,

(*JOLANDA THE VIRGIN OF THE BRONX, light on her.*)

Your parking attendants, your

(Pictures of cast in those outfits is a collage.)

Writers, your workers, your executives,

(Picture of the MANIC HISPANIC, the film executive is seen on the wall.)

Your employees, your entertainers, your Border Patrol Agents.

(Light on BUFORD GOMEZ as he speaks)

We are all this and much more. We are . . . *Latinologues*!

Rest easy, Erazmo and good night everybody!

(Then BUFORD GOMEZ freezes. Lights out.)

(Then lights up, cast come back up and cast holds hands and takes their bow and then the cast leaves the stage.)

(A smiling picture of ERAZMO washing dishes or working is on the wall.)

(BLACK OUT.)

Above: Cast and crew spend hours in rehearsal before each production.

Above (l. to r.): Susie Albin-Najera and Rick L. Najera are joined by Delilah Cotto and René Lavan at the Los Angeles production.

Above (l.–r.): Mike Robles, Quentin Taratino and friend, Rick L.Najera and Fernando Carrillo after a performance of Latinologues.

Left: A sample of the mind-boggling touring schedule for Latinologues.

RICK NAJERA'S LATINOLOGUES™

3-31	SAN LUIS OBISPO	CHRISTOPHER COHAN CENTER	805-756-2787	PACSLO.ORG
4-1	LANCASTER	LANCASTER PERFORMING ARTS CENTER	661-723-5950	LPAC.ORG
4-2	FRESNO	WILLIAM SAROYAN THEATER	559-485-8497	TICKETMASTER.COM
4-3	SACRAMENTO	THE CREST THEATRE	916-768-2277	TICKETS.COM
4-7	SEATTLE	THE MOORE THEATER	206-628-0888	TICKETMASTER.COM
4-8	PORTLAND	THE NEWMARK THEATER	503-224-4400	TICKETMASTER.COM
4-8	SANTA BARBARA	ARLINGTON THEATER	805-963-4408	TICKETMASTER.COM
4-14	DALLAS	MAJESTIC THEATER	214-373-8000	TICKETMASTER.COM
4-15	DALLAS	MAJESTIC THEATER	214-373-8000	TICKETMASTER.COM
4-16	HOUSTON	VERIZON WIRELESS THEATER	713-629-3700	TICKETMASTER.COM
4-17	AUSTIN	PARAMOUNT THEATRE	866-4GET-TIX	GETTIX.NET
4-22	LAREDO	LAREDO CIVIC CENTER	956-794-1700	TICKETMASTER.COM
4-23	HARLIGEN	MUNICIPAL AUDITORIUM	TICKETS AVAILABLE AT THE BOX OFFICE	
4-24	HARLIGEN	MUNICIPAL AUDITORIUM	TICKETS AVAILABLE AT THE BOX OFFICE	
4-28	GREELY	MONFORT HALL AT UNION COLONY C.C.	800-315 ARTS	UCSTARS.COM
4-29	DENVER	PARAMOUNT THEATER	303-830-TIXS	TICKETMASTER.COM
4-30	ALBUQUERQUE	KIVA AUDITORIUM	505-883-7800	TICKETMASTER.COM
5-1	EL PASO	ABRAHAM CHAVEZ CENTER	915-532-4661	TICKETMASTER.COM
5-2	RIVERSIDE	MUNICIPAL AUDITORIUM	714-740-2000	TICKETMASTER.COM
5-3	BAKERSFIELD	FOX THEATER	661-322-5200	VALLITIX.COM
6-4	STOCKTON	BOB HOPE THEATER	209-337-4673	BOBHOPETHEATER.COM
6-5	OXNARD	OXNARD PERFORMING ARTS CENTER	805-486-2424	ETIX.COM

LATINOLOGUES.NET ICONCONCERTS.COM

Photo by Susie Albin-Najera

Left: Backstage scene as the cast preps for a big show.

Below: The Najera kids, often join their dad on tour (l. to r.): Sonora, Kennedy and Julian.

Photo by Susie Albin-Najera

Photo by Susie Albin-Najera

Above: Actor and hip-hop artist Unik (left) guest-starred in the New York production of Latinologues.

Right: Broadway playwright and author of Latinologues, *Rick L. Najera, doing press in New York.*

MÁS MONOLOGUES

PLAYWRIGHT'S NOTES

*"Imagine an America without immigrants and
you can imagine all of you gone."*
—Rick Najera, Latins Anonymous

These are monologues that have been performed over the years and we performed them at a special 15-year anniversary show at the Ricardo Montalban Theatre in Hollywood. What was odd about it was we did it with no advertising, just a Facebook blast and over 750 people showed up that night. *Latinologues* had come into the modern Facebook age. When I started this play, I had never even sent an email. These monologues were added to the show that night. It was our 15-year anniversary of *Latinologues*. This was our *quinceañera*. But at this *quinceañera* there was no strange uncle who was still living at his mom's house who wanted to dance close to the *quince* girl and sing along to the oldie's song, "Let's get it on." And at that *quince* celebration no one had a gun. I told the audience why I wrote these additional monologues.

—Rick L. Najera

FOREWORD

BY RAFAEL AGUSTÍN

With the release of the new Federal Census, many Americans are barely now discovering what all of us from the beautiful barrios around the nation already knew: Latinos procreate like nobody's business! Fifty million strong! We are the largest minority group in the U.S., primed and ready to take on the role of the majority within a few decades. Why is this relevant? Our sheer numbers make us more than just a powerful voting block or a sought after consumer market, it makes us the new America.

Rick Najera has been writing for this new America for over two decades now. He was "Latin" at a time when most Latinos with his skin color passed as white and "Latino" when the local political movement demanded he be Chicano. Najera wrote for our community when the national political climate demanded we focus on the "Me" and made us laugh at a time when immigration policies were at their saddest. Rick Najera paved the way for all of us Latinos who followed in his footsteps into the maddening world of Hollywood—and he did so alone, in a dark room with just simply his thoughts and a typewriter (yes, he's been around that long!)

I first discovered Rick Najera's work while attending Mt. San Antonio College. How I ended up at my local community college was a testament to the new America that was looming at the time. I had just finished high school having been the Senior Class President, the Prom King and in the top 10 percent of my class. I was the All-American high school student with one small exception: I was not American at all; at least not according to my immigration status. I had no Social Security number; only a Tax

ID number that was provided to me by the federal government. I became what the *L.A. Times* would later dub "the underground undergrad," an undocumented student immigrant. With school tuition on the rise, I ended up at the only place I could afford, community college—a place I saw as my holding cell until I resolved my immigration issues.

Luckily for me, community college became my greatest source of knowledge and education. I include my later work as a graduate student in this equation, but I didn't know that at the time. At the time I thought I was condemned to never leave this place of "lower learning," so I took every class available to me to pass the time: Philosophy, Astronomy, World Religions, Film Studies, Anthropology, Statistics, Literature, Chemistry, Biology, Theater . . . Theater. What a strange little world I had accidently stumbled into. Here was a place where I would be praised and awarded for convincingly playing someone I was not. I had been acting like an American since the day I came to this country at the age of seven. Acting was what I did best!

It was my community college theater professor who asked me to go to this cult-like bookstore called Samuel French for the first time. Samuel French was the first time that I had ever ventured out of "East, East LA" (West Covina, CA) and into Hollywood. The Sunset Strip felt like an entirely different world, just a few miles from my actual home. The bookstore itself was a theater freak's wet-dream. There were plays, compilations, monologue books and specialty books. One of these specialty books that I found in the ethnic section was *Pain of the Macho*, by Rick Najera. The humor and heartbreak that pour out of these Latino-centric tirades spoke to me unlike anything else I had ever read in a play. He took the stereotypes I had begrudgingly gotten accustomed to playing (janitor, mechanic, gangster, etc.) and made them three dimensional characters. These monologues about the struggles and joy of being Latino were very familiar to me because they were written in the voices of people I knew too well: the ambitious immigrant, the egotistical college professor, the misunderstood gang member, the overzealous busboy. These characters spoke for us and about us. Writer and literary critic Harold Bloom argued that Shakespeare "invented" humanity, in that he prescribed the now-common practice of "overhearing" ourselves, which drives our changes. I argue that Rick Najera "invented" the Latino, in that his comedy and poignancy drives our communal understanding of who we are and what we are capable of.

Years later, I found myself performing next to Rick Najera at the Latino Laugh Festival which was held at the Kodak Theater. I was performing in my new comedy N*GGER WETB*CK CH*NK. He was promoting his comedy staple *Latinologues*. It was at this festival that Rick revealed to me that *Pain of the Macho* served as the blueprint to his greater work that he had since dubbed *Latinologues*.

From headlining on the Las Vegas Strip, to standing ovations and sold out crowds, *Latinologues* has toured the nation and received rave reviews such as 'Top Pick," "Recommended" and "Critics Choice" from theater critics nationwide. The show has also received numerous accolades and official commendations from City Mayors and U.S. Senators for its production and was awarded an Imagen Award for Best Live Theatrical Production. Each monologue delivered is meant to educate, inspire and most of all make you laugh. The show is and remains to be a true service to the Latino community.

Latinologues made its Broadway debut in September 2005 at the legendary Helen Hayes Theatre with an initial 12-week engagement, plus an additional four-week extension by popular demand. The Broadway show was directed by the legendary comedian, Cheech Marin, and featured Rick Najera, Eugenio Derbez, Rene Lavan and Shirley A. Rumierk. From the well-known and most-loved character, Buford Gomez, who provides a comprehensive seminar on efficient Border Patrol tactics, to Miss Puerto Rican Day Pride Parade who will do anything to save her crown, to Fidel who outsmarts "La Migra" and heads to Puerto Vallarta for free. Other characters include "Alejandro" the heartthrob bus boy who is mesmerized by a blonde, the unstoppable and radical MEChA members who fight to create justice ("I may be radical but don't call after ten, my mom gets mad") to the *Manic Hispanic* Hollywood Producer, which the *Houston Chronicle* called "Charles Nelson Riley dipped in salsa."

Latinologues has provided education and mentorship to hundreds of actors and has launched the professional careers for dozens of Latinos. More than 150 different guest performers have participated in the show throughout the years. From the unknown to the famous, *Latinologues* has been home to such stars as Eugenio Derbez, Edward James Olmos, Jaime Camil, Cynthia Klitbo, Eric Estrada, Geraldo Rivera, Christina, Maria Conchita Alonso, Jacob Vargas, Mario Lopez, Cristian De La

Fuente, Fernando Carrillo, Rene Lavan Gabriel Iglesias, Emilio Rivera, Yareli Arizmendi and Gene Pompa. In 2009, I became part of the *Latinologues* legacy by performing next to Rick at the Hayworth Theater for six months and then again at its 15th-year anniversary in 2010 at the Montalban Theatre.

No other living writer today best captures the warmth, humor, pain, triumph and humility of the Latino experience than Rick Najera. The Latino Tyler Perry, this literary giant will continue to write as long as our culture continues to strive, prosper and laugh.

Imagine a Hollywood without Rick Najera and you can imagine all of us . . . gone.

—Rafael Agustín

(Rafael Agustín is the co-creator of the award-winning play *N*GGER WETB*CK CH*NK* and has been a producer and actor in *Latinologues* for three years.)

INTRODUCTION TO

MÁS MONOLOGUES

One day I heard a voice, it was a quiet voice; it was the voice of God. I heard "Rick, Rick, Rick." I was amazed. Then I said, "God is that you?" And God said, "Oh, I'm sorry. I was looking for a different Rick. I mistook you from the back. You look just like that other Rick that I needed to talk to. I was looking for Rick Sanchez. He's going to go on and do great things at CNN then get fired. I don't have any real plans for you, Rick. Forget I ever called your name. Well, see you in 40 years. Oh, invest in gold."

It was then that I decided to do something big. I wanted to create a show to showcase Latinos in the United States. Sometimes people would get angry because they thought I was making fun of our community. In actuality, I was celebrating our community. After a show in Portland, Oregon, a Latino man in a red velour jacket with a pinky ring came up to me and said, "You should not write about stereotypes or people with accents. I'm Mexican and it offends me. You should show nice Latinos and you should do the show with more Spanish. Don't show stereotypes." I looked at him in amazement and said, "You're in a red velour jacket, with gold jewelry, gold teeth and a thick accent. I could not have made you up; you are a stereotype." It was the truth. Then he asked me to give him an autograph for his kids. I asked him what their names were. He said, "Jonathan and Stephanie Ramirez." I cannot make this stuff up. And we were in Oregon. We are a complicated people.

With *Latinologues*, I wanted to tell our stories. I think more than a 150 actors have been in this show. It's been a joy.

The first monologues I ever wrote were what I call "Barrio Stories," those stories that I saw happening within the community all around me. But with this next set of monologues, I wanted to tell a few more stories and say what was left unsaid. These are *Más Monologues.*

Alejandro and *Jolanda* were the first two monologues that I wrote. But the first monologue I ever performed was this one called *Wetback.* It was from my show, *Latins Anonymous,* and it goes like this . . .

—Rick L. Najera

WETBACK

RICK (*in character:*)

Hi, my name is Rick and I admit I'm a Latino. I first realized I was Latino when I was nine years old. A kid named Brad came up to me and called me a wetback. I had never heard the term before. Wetback. It didn't sound like a bad word: full back, half back, quarter back, wetback. But just to play it safe, I kicked his ass. So then this teacher ran up to me and said, "Why did you beat up Bradley?" And I said, "Because he called me a wetback." Then she said, "Are you Mexican?" I said, "Yes." And she said, "Well you *are* a wetback."

(*Lights change back.*)

RICK (*as himself:*)

That is a true story. And that was in San Diego in my little racist school on the prairie. That incident shaped my world. But that was years ago. Now there are no prejudices or cultural issues or biases; it's one big Kumbaya song and everything's O.K. in the world. Things are OK. Except in Arizona. Oh, and there are tons of Latinos on TV . . . In Univison and in bikinis with little people and in Spanish for less money. OK, I guess we got some work still to do. So from that incident at my elementary school to Broadway, I wrote about people and places I knew about; some good, some bad, but all very human. And that is the beginning of this story. These are the barrio stories.

(LIGHTS OUT.)

PAQUITO

(Lights up. PAQUITO enters from the back of the house.)

PAQUITO: *(To audience:)*

Man, I love being here at the Latin Grammys. It's a dream come true.

(Onstage)

(He stops and eagerly addresses Latin star Enrique Iglesias.)

Enrique Iglesias, Enrique . . . How are you man? Great song, I love it . . . Wait. *(Singing.)* "I could be your hero baby; I could take away the pain, oh yeah." Great song huh. You and John Secada should form a girl band man.

(Responding to a question.)

It's me, Paquito from Menudo. Remember me?

(To audience:)

I'm telling you, its great being here at the Latin Grammys even though I'm the bar back in charge of ice.

(Removes jacket to reveal a Cuervo apron as a Cuervo box is pushed onstage.)

You know refrigeration is very important scientific work for the stars you know. Because you really . . .

(He stops mid-sentence and eagerly addresses Latin star Ricky Martin.)

Ricky Martin! Ricky Martin. Ricky, how are you man? Good to see you. Remember me? We used to work together, Ricky. Come and dance with me, man like we used to in the old days, brother.

(Menudo's 1981 hit "Fuego" plays. PAQUITO dances.)

What? Get you a daiquiri? I piss in your daiquiri and I piss in your piña colada, man.

(To audience:)

I used to be somebody you know. I was a member of the greatest band in the history of music, Menudo. We were like the Beatles, but browner and with thicker accents. Those were the days, you know? I had everything a teenage boy could ever want—cars, fame, and boys. I mean voice, like singing voice. But then you turn 16 and they kick you out. I was the only idiot who gave my real age. Ay Menudo, Menudo, Menudo. Those were the days, I'm telling you.

(Menudo's "Ven a Volar" plays. PAQUITO dances. Suddenly he stops, grabbing his hip.)

Ahhh! Ahhh! Pelvic arthritis. Walk it out brother, walk it out.

(He walks it out.)

I remember when my manager found me. I had lots of money back then. My manager invested in good investments, real estate. And I'm telling you, they were good. His house has tripled in value already. But for me, he invested in solid investments like . . . a beautiful, beautiful ski lodge in Puerto Rico. But it never snowed. Pac Man videos, the Michael Dukakis campaign. I traveled the world and I played to packed audiences. But on my 16th birthday, my manager came in with this little mocoso kid, who looked at me and said, "Who's the old man?" Old Man! And I knew something was wrong because I started feeling the beard on my face. And it wasn't my manager's beard, or any of his friends. It was my own beard growing from my own face. I knew it was over. So I said to the little *mocoso* kid, "Listen, Chayan. Or whatever your tribal name is, you're not Indian. And you are not Menudo material. And you will never amount to anything." *(Beat)* I guess I was wrong. You know the funny thing; he was never even in Menudo. He was in Chico, or Chamos or some shit like that. I felt like a Latino Gary Coleman, only not so angry, and with no reality show. I was washed up at 16. Lots of memories, physical pain, mental scars, shot vocal chords. This is a very common disease in Puerto Rico. It's called PMSS. Post Menudo Shock Syndrome. But I got no regrets. I'm working here at the Latin Grammys. And there will be more Latin shows to work on in the future because we are in and we are hip.

(Shakes his hips then stops in pain.)

Although I might need a new hip. I guess I'm doing alright.

(He stops mid-thought and eagerly addresses Latin star Juan Gabriel.)

Juan Gabriel! Oh my God, Juan Gabriel. Looking good man. That's a fancy walker you got there man. What can I get you? Sex on the Beach? Right away. *(Beat)* But what would you like to drink?

(To audience:)

I used to be somebody. Yeah. I am somebody.

(Menudo's smash hit "Súbete A Mi Moto" plays. PAQUITO dances.)

(Lights dim as he dances off stage.)

EAST L.A. BAYWATCH

(BIG JOKER, an East Los Angeles lifeguard at a kiddy pool walks to center stage. We hear splashing. Kids play in the background. BIG JOKER is training some unseen recruits.)

BIG JOKER: *(TO AUDIENCE, INTO BULLHORN:)*

Okay, life guards and all you recruits, you are at the East L.A. Kiddy Pool and even though it's only three feet deep, this is still the most dangerous assignment in the city.

(Puts the bullhorn down.)

This ain't no Malibu public pool; this shit is for real. You're in East L.A. That pool is three feet deep and crowded and got *manteca* stains around the edges, but it's home.

(To swimmers, into bullhorn:)

Hey, you Cuban kids! Share the raft! Hey, drowning kid! Just stand up, it's only three feet deep. Stupid.

(Puts the bullhorn down.)

(To audience:)

Listen up. We don't use chlorine, we use bleach. We don't have undertow, we got camel toe. We don't have sharks, we got sexual predators and they will follow you home.

This is your equipment.

(He holds up milk cartons.)

Because of budget cuts we just have plastic milk bottles tied around our arms. These are our water wings. We ain't got no money because our governor may be in good shape but financially, we're flabby. And the mayor, he's a player like my dad. He's got three car payments and three girlfriends; he's got no money either. 'Cause we're so broke my dad took me and my sister to the I-Hop for her *quinceañera*. I had to say I was nine so I could eat for free. And they were suspicious of us because I drove there. It was embarrassing. So we have to pay for our own equipment. All we got is our regulation swim trunks and our skills to survive. But don't get scared, just remember: It's only three feet deep, so just stand up and you can make it.

(To swimmer, into bullhorn:)

Hey, Paco. What are those, cutoff Dickeys? I think a dickey is hanging out of your Dickeys. Buy yourself some swimming trunks already. What's that in the pool? That isn't a Snickers bar. *Cochinos.*

(Puts the bullhorn down.)

(To audience:)

This place is dangerous. We got visual dangers, like that fat Mexican guy there, wearing a Speedo. Damn look at him, he looks like a *platano* in a hammock. Hey, mister! It looks like your ass is eating your *chonies*. You spoiled my lunch. You owe me a happy meals cause I ain't happy looking at your ass. That Speedo is like a wonder Speedo, when I see him in it, I don't have to wonder.

Here is a little warning for you new girls. Don't rescue Melody; she just got out of prison. Never give mouth-to-mouth to an ex-con. They get too clingy. You start getting collect calls from prison. I ain't got that kind of money. I know what you're thinking. How do I stand the pressure of being an East L.A. Kiddy Pool lifeguard? The constant life and death . . . ? Well, drinking this 40-ouncer helps.

(She pulls out a 40-ounce can of beer and cracks it open.)

THIS HELPS. BIG TIME. One for me, one for my homies.

(She drinks once for her, and she pours one drink on the ground.)

I'll miss you, Grandma. I told you not to hang out on the porch at night in gang colors. It was an Asian gang in a Toyota. She was hooked to the bumper in her walker. It was a Prius; she was dragged nearly 500 miles before they stopped for gas . . .

What I do here may not be by the book, because I can't read, but it works. I provide a valuable service for the Parks—and I'm not talking about the Korean family that swims here. Parks and Recreation. I remember when I started here years ago; I had big dreams. I wanted to get a job as a waitress at Hooters or at least make enough money to get a boob job to work at Hooters. But life throws little curves at you, like . . . prison, or like drunk driving records. Or bad credit. Or no credit. Or in my case, using someone else's credit. And, of course, the three strikes law. I stole a pizza and I almost got life.

(To swimmer, into bullhorn:)

Hey, Dominican kid, get in the pool. Why you scared for? I saw that movie, *Pride*, about the black swim team. Your people can swim. I also saw that movie, *The Blind Side*, which taught me another lesson: that pushy white woman can pick a number one draft pick. Hey, you *elote* guy, stop washing your clothes in the pool. What's wrong with you? Get out of the pool. *(Puts the bullhorn down.)*

(To audience:)

But there are perks working here, such as all the jewelry you can find on the bottom of the pool, or in lockers, or unattended cars in the parking lot.

(To swimmer:)

Hey, *elote* guy! Stop washing your rooster in the pool.

(To audience:)

Damn cock-fighting fools. Man, that's ghetto.

(To swimmer:)

I got 20 on him!

(To audience:)

Except if he fights a Filipino rooster. Man, ever since Paquito came around all these Filipino roosters got brave.

Okay recruits, I think you all are ready. Welcome to East L.A. Kiddy Pool. This completes your four minutes of official training, so good luck. You're now officially lifeguards. But one last thing, a lot of people are going to look at you and say, "Why aren't you in Santa Monica with all their wave runners, professional boats and Jeeps . . . with working headlights?" Well when people say, "Why are you here in the barrio in a public kiddy pool?" Well this is what I tell them, "Because I got a sense of pride. And this kiddy pool is the last refuge for our community."

My grandma was denied access here when she was a little girl because it used to be a Whites-Only swimming pool. Now look at us. We saved this pool. Latinos are saving all the public areas that Americans no longer use and let go to waste. So, no, I don't want to go to Santa Monica. I want to stay here in East L.A. because if the hood had more people of quality staying here as opposed to leaving when they get all educated and paid, then our community might be better off. That's why I stayed…

That and I got a DUI so I can't drive that far. And those public busses, they smell like piss and broken dreams. So forget it. Now go out there and save lives.

Photo by Jesse Garcia

(To swimmer:)

What? Save you? I ain't getting my clothes wet. You better stand up because I ain't calling 911. I ran out of minutes fool. Besides I'm on break . . .

(To audience:)

Good luck.

(She exits. Lights out.)

Carmen Corral and Momo Rodriguez in East L.A. Baywatch.

SUNSET OF MY CAREER

INTRODUCTION

The Latino experience runs the gamet: everything from La Sad Girl at a kiddy pool in "East Los," to the first Latina astronaut, Ellen Ochoa—who strangely enough was from my neighborhood. She used to get high . . . grades in science.

I loved growing up in California. At that time there were no Latinos, there were just Mexicans. There were no El Salvadorians.

(First time I heard "eat my *pupusa*" I was shocked. But I ate her *pupusa*. It was delicious.)

I grew up on the border, 15 miles from Tijuana. The real border for many Latinos has been Hollywood. Our stories have been seldom told and when they are, they are not told by Latinos.

In the 15 years that I've been doing this show, I've cast more Latinos in leading roles than most major networks combined in any season: 150 to be exact. Fifteen years ago there were more dinosaurs in leading roles on television than Latinos, until the George Lopez Show. (But he got replaced by the cavemen from the insurance commercials.) Who says Hollywood does not care about minorities? But Hollywood is what America exports to the world. It's our images and sometimes lack of these monologues that I call "Hollywood Stories."

—Rick L. Najera

SUNSET OF MY CAREER

(Lights up. A scream is heard from off-stage. Moments later an actress, clearly at the end of her career, runs onstage holding a telephone. She dons a starlet's gown and her make-up is overdone. This is MISS EAST SUNSET BOULEVARD.)

MISS EAST *(Into phone)*: Operator, operator. I just shot a man. Where do I live? East Sunset Boulevard, in La Puente. Wait! What do you mean I have to hold? *(Beat)*

OPERATOR *(Heard as a voiceover)*: For gunshot incidents, please press one. For all other emergencies, please press three. If you are a victim, stay on the line. If you have been shot multiple times, seek medical attention. If you have been shot just one time then come on! Man up, *puto*! Walk it off!

MISS EAST *(Into phone)*: Police, please. I just shot a man. I shot him. He was a Latino writer—I know rare. Rare like a faithful Latino man rare. Rare like a Latino film opening at a Latino Film festival. Rare like organic tofu chorizo. Well now he's extinct. He's extinct. *(Beat)*

I live on East Sunset Boulevard in East L.A. *(Beat)* Yes, I killed him. He was living with me in my two-bedroom stucco mansion. I caught my man writing for another Latina actress. I caught him writing a spec script for Eva Longoria, that little *Desperate Housewife*. I'm more desperate than she will ever be. *(Beat)* Yes, I did shoot him. Send an ambulance. He's dead, so take your time. Please bring paparazzi. You'll recognize me.

(To audience:)

I know I look familiar. I was a very famous actress once when Hollywood was full of raw energy and paved with golden dreams. When *"nosotros"* meant "us."

I played a *chola* in some of the most famous gang movies ever to hit the VHS market. My gang films were classy, riveting and even more intriguing than Jenna Jameson's. Although gang banging wasn't as violent in my films. I never got shot in the face. That meant something entirely different in my films. Now you remember me? I was in *Resurrection Boulevard.* I was the melodramatic Latina with dark hair . . . ? And dark eyes . . . ? But then again, so was every other Latina actor ever known to man. In the good old days when Maria Conchita was running with Arnold Schwarzenegger in spandex. I was in the George Lopez show, playing George Lopez's stand in—we both have a huge head. I looked like a Mexican lollipop, but less bitter. Come on, George you're America's highest paid Mexican. Be happy. I played an El Salvadorian maid. I was an immigrant in a successful off, off, off Broadway play in Michigan entitled, *Illegal on a Hot Tin Roof.* My credits are as long as I have been unemployed. I won a Cuban-American Arts Award, the CACA award. My performance was *"puro caca"* the *Republican Cuban Times* said. Thank you, Miami. I know most of you know me from my signature role in the *Rosarito Refried Bean Woman* story. Not at the film at Cannes, but on the can of beans. Don't remember?

(To MAX, offstage:)

MAX! Max, get me a can of Rosarito Refried Beans! And some Indian braids and brown tanning spray. I want to practice.

(MAX, an elderly Latino butler, enters.)

MAX *(To Miss East)*: Yes, my lady. Ya full, madam?

MISS EAST *(To audience)*: Max is my director. He's Argentinean.

(To MAX:)

Stop with your accent, you're not European. You are Argentinean, you are not European.

MAX: Yes, my lady.

MISS EAST: Have the police arrived?

MAX: No, I am afraid not my lady.

MISS EAST: They're not coming? *(Beat)* Max.

MAX: No, madam!

MISS EAST *(To audience:)* So, here I am in Hollywood. Not working. Hollywood is out of touch by not having any good roles for Latinas. And when they are good, they are not played by a Latina. Or worse yet, played by a real Mexican millionaire actress trying to cross over. Damn you, Kate del Castillo! I lost a role to a Lebanese woman once. Damn you, Salma Hayek! Maybe I should have loved my Latino writer—they are rare in Hollywood. But now he's extinct. I had to kill him. You loved me once. Remember me? I made you hot and bothered and it wasn't just lipstick. You like me. You really like me.

(To MAX:)

Max, has anybody arrived?

MAX: No one's coming, madam.

MISS EAST: Okay, wrap him up in aluminum foil and put him next to the Christmas tamales. Put him on ice because nobody's coming. Nobody's coming.

MAX: Oh hello no, madam. Nobody's coming.

Photo by Jesse Garcia

MISS EAST: I'm ready for my close up, Frank Reyes. I'm available; too available, on East Sunset Boulevard in La Puente.

(LIGHTS OUT.)

Dyana Ortelli as Miss East in Sunset of My Career.

EX-TELENOVELA STAR THALIA

(We hear a doorbell then lights up on a very good-looking young woman. Her clothing is form fitting, sexy and revealing—cleavage, legs and all. Her name is THALIA. She speaks with a thick Spanish accent. She is an ex-telenovela star she holds a suitcase)

THALIA: *(To audience:)*

Hello, nice to meet you Ms. Bolter. I'm Thalia. I have been hired to be the new nanny. *(Beat)* The nanny in your house. This very house right here. You look surprised. I thought your husband told you. I was supposed to start after you left for your home in Nantucket for the summer. He said I would start living and working here then but I thought I'd come here early.

Wow, you look really surprised. He didn't tell you? Well I was even more surprised when he hired me. Because I have no real experience with children or anything to do with kids. I can't cook. I can't clean. And the only jobs on my résumé were lingerie model and *telenovela*. He said he loved my potential. I came to the United States to work in Hollywood. And then when I met your husband at Starbucks, or his office as he calls it, he started asking me questions and talking to me. I told him I was looking for a job. Then, well here I am! He said he had a job for me.

Yes, I'm an actress too. More good news, I know. I was in *telenovelas* in Mexico. I liked being a *telenovela* star. I was in *Dos Hermanos, So Little Time*. I came to the United States to cross over, and I'm not just talking the Tijuana border. I was born to act. You have to study hard to be a *telenovela* actress. But now that I came to the United States I'm going to make it. I took English and accent reduction classes. I don't even sound Latina anymore. I studied hard in school. I can do accents.

I can do Swedish. *(Her accent does not change.)*

"Hello, how are you?"

I can do French. *(Her accent does not change.)*

"Hello, how are you?"

I can do Russian. *(Her accent does not change.)*

"Hello, how are you?"

I studied in New York with a Puerto Rican methadone actor. So I'm ready. And having a job as your nanny will free me up to audition for shows. I love romance and fantasy. *Telenovelas* are fantasy because most of my leading men were more interested in the other leading men than in me. It's true. People love fantasy because life is so boring. But in *telenovelas*, life is fascinating. One minute you're a humble Indian maid. The next minute you are married to a rich plastic surgeon and part-time nuclear scientist.

The Hindus believe you are born more than once—but if you work in a 7-Eleven store you have to dream. I don't believe that. I went to a psychic who said I had all these past lives, but in every past life I was royalty. No one is that lucky. Back in the past, jobs were bad. Back then they gave out jobs, like eunuchs. It was rough getting that job. Being a eunuch was bad. It was like working the night shift at the post office, but with no balls. I'd hate to tell a guy great news . . .

(To young guy:)

"Hey, Habi, you are working in the king's harem but you'll need to leave your balls behind in your locker." You have a beautiful pool I can't wait to go swimming in that pool. I used to model bikinis so I have lots of old swimsuits.

I miss my old life. I miss Mexico City. There are 13 million people living there. People ask me how the government takes care of 13 million people. I say, "Easy, they only care for about 12 of them." It's not easy to be an ex-*telenovela* star and moving to America. But now that I got the job as your new nanny, I feel like I'm home.

So where is Mr. Bolter? *(Beat)*

Oh, really . . . Seriously? The job has been filled? You don't need me? Oh, really? Wow. Now I'm surprised. No, don't worry. I'll let myself out. I knew it was too good to be true . . . just like a *telenovela*.

(LIGHTS OUT.)

INSIDE THE PORN ACTOR'S STUDIO

INTRODUCTION

This new sketch was performed recently at the Conga Room in a *Latinologues.* It was an audience favorite.

—Rick L Najera

INSIDE THE PORN ACTOR'S STUDIO

(An ASSISTANT dressed in jeans and a t-shirt, scrambles around on stage setting up three chairs center-stage. A projected slide on the stages screen reads "Inside the Porn Actor's Studio.")

Graphics by Momo Rodriguez

ASSISTANT: Are you ready? We're on in . . . five, four, three . . .

(The host walks out onto the stage and stands before the chair furthest stage right. He sounds and looks remarkably like James Lipton.)

ASSISTANT: . . . Two, one! *(Points to the host and runs offstage.)*

HOST: *(To audience:)*

Welcome to the 15th Annual *Imagine We Are Successful Awards.* The *Imagine We Are Successful Awards*—sponsored by many white liberal people—loves to give back to the community. And this actress—I am not ashamed to say—I have been dying to get inside . . . her mind. It must be warm and tight and filled with so much experience. So many juicy, wet experiences. So many Latino actors are not used in Hollywood. *But,* where Latino Actors *are* being used is in pornography.

Today we have with us some of the real pioneers and stars in Latino porn. First off, let me introduce a woman who was honored with the award in our new category, Best Latina Actress in a Porn Film for 2011.

This Latina has opened doors and her legs and sometimes if paid enough, her back door, to be a porn star. She made it into an art form. Please give it up ladies and gentleman because she gives it up—on film—for Sweet Candy Marquez, or as she is called in the barrio, "Dulce" Panocha Marquez!

(A Latina female walks onto the stage. She is dressed extremely provocatively sporting clothing and jewelry that is "blinged out" and "hooker heels." Her hair is large and teased. A proud smile is plastered across her face. The projected slide changes to a slide with PANOCHA MARQUEZ's name and logo plastered across it.)

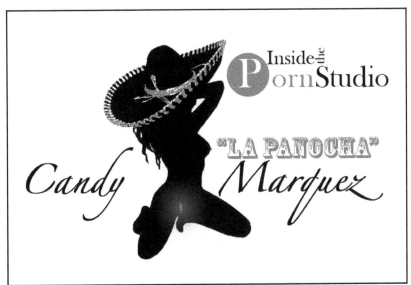

Inside the PornStudio

"LA PANOCHA"

Candy Marquez

Graphics by Momo Rodriguez

VANESSA: *(To audience:)*

Gracias, I want to thank God.

HOST: *(To Vanessa:)*

Uh, really? God?

VANESSA: *(To host:)*

Yeah. I constantly call out to God while I'm working.

(To audience:) "Oh god, oh god! It feels so good . . . to have this career. *(She smiles.)*

HOST: *(To Vanessa:)*

OK.

(To audience:)

Also joining us on stage tonight, her partner and co-star in *Dancing with the Porn Stars,* Fernando "El Tripod" Toledo.

(FERNANDO walks out onto the stage. He sports sunglasses, a tacky gold chain and '70's porn-wear. As he stops before the chair furthest stage left, he places his right foot atop it. An obviously extremely large penis runs down the length of his thigh. He rubs it periodically throughout the sketch as they speak.)

FERNANDO: *(To audience:)*

It's great to be on the show. Vanessa is a real role model. She encountered prejudice and overcame it, so that any Latina could work in the porn industry and be treated equally. At the end of any line of porn actors, I can't wait to work with her again—as soon as I'm cleared medically to work. I thought positive was a good thing.

(Smiles, poses and rubs his penis)

VANESSA: *(To audience:)*

Thank you. This is about rights. Porn women's rights. Grace Kelly did everything Fred Astaire did, but backwards and in heels. Well, I did everything John Holmes did, but in heels, a whip, chain, a dog collar around my neck and a plug up my . . .

HOST: *(To Vanessa, cutting her off:)*

Exactly.

VANESSA: My point is, I'm honored.

HOST: Yes. You double penetrated your way into this industry with talent and determination. But why was it so difficult?

VANESSA: Type casting. I was always the maid getting screwed and never the astronaut.

FERNANDO: I was always a gangbanger. I can play more than that. I got range and a big talent.

(Smiles, poses and rubs his penis)

VANESSA: But I changed all that. I was an oceanographer in *Dive on This*. I was a cop in *You're Under My Dress*. I was the first Latina to do all those things, but has any Latino organization ever given me an award? Only the Imagen Foundation, but who really cares about them? And that was only because I bought a table and an ad and I was nice to the old Venezuelan guy who runs it. He made me dress up like Chavez . . .

FERNANDO: She was great in *ER All over My Face* where she played a head surgeon. That was the best film of the year, for real. But watch out for me in my new film *Conception*. It will blow your mind. We filmed it in 3-D. And warning, the first rows at the theater may get wet. Wear protection. Wear a raincoat.

(Smiles, poses and rubs his penis)

VANESSA: He's always plugging himself. I want to thank my manager Jerry Goldfarbmenstine Rodriguez. I want to thank my Cuban manager and ex-boyfriend. We were together for two wonderful days at his house before his wife came home. That bitch got all dramatic! She's the one that should win an award . . . for *drama*. Just because you're married and have four kids does not mean you own him. And bitch, give me back my earrings. I know you have them because I saw you wearing them on Facebook.

FERNANDO: Jerry is great. He got me the job on a special episode of *Dangerous Catch*. Being on that crab boat was hard . . . But nobody knows how to catch crabs like me.

(Smiles, poses and rubs his penis.)

HOST: *(To Vanessa:)*

Why aren't there more Spanish-language porn stars being honored? Isn't it harder to act in porn in Spanish?

VANESSA: It is harder to do porn in Spanish. Because it's hard to roll your R's when your mouth is full. Let's be honest, we're not tossing Caesar salads here. We're tossing CEZARRR salads—CEZARRR. *(Rolling her r's.)*

And it's true that Spanish-language porn is tougher, because it's more emotional. Spanish is a romance language and there is nothing more romantic than the Spanish-language porn film *Amorous Doggy Style*. *(Smiles)* And I still do Spanish-language porn . . . My grandma, she doesn't speak English.

HOST: Right. You want to keep it in the familia.

VANESSA: Exactly. So I still do Spanish-language porn, it just pays less. And let's be honest, when you're getting the *pito*, you don't want to be getting the *peso*. You want to be getting the dollar, you know what I'm saying? You can check out my work this month in the Latino Film festival where I'll act in Spanish. I'll be in *Y Tu Mama Gives Head* and *La Misma Puna* or in English *Under the Same Pune*. Oh! And I want to give a shout out to the mayor, Antonio Villaraigosa. I received a key to the city from the mayor . . . but he said it only works on his condo in Hollywood. But still, it's a key!

HOST: *(To Vanessa:)*

Future plans?

VANESSA: I have my own line of Latino porn products.

(The projected slide changes to a slide displaying her product line.)

Graphics by Momo Rodriguez

Limon Con Chili Lube—it's hot, spicy and sexy; ostrich skin condoms—for her pleasure; and Banda booty beads. Dangles sold separately.

HOST: You are a delight. Thank you so much for giving so much of your self . . . to your community.

FERNANDO: *(To host/audience:)*

She's like the Dominican Republica. Hot, steamy and cheap to visit. But more than that, she is an activist.

(To Vanessa/audience:)

Don't be shy. Tell him about your work at the border. *(Smiles, poses and rubs his penis.)*

VANESSA: I started the Deep Throaters against Borders.

(Lifts fist and shouts.)

¡Sí se puede! The Deep Throaters against Borders is important and dear to me because us porn performers never close our borders or refuse entrance to anyone. Because there is nothing ever closed on me.

(Parting her legs.)

I am open and ready to receive immigrants. I love this job and whatever the winds blow, I'll blow even harder.

FERNANDO: And watch out for her special on Animal Planet, *The Donkey Whisperer.*

(Smiles, poses and rubs his penis.)

HOST: *(To himself:)*

This is so wrong. *(Beat)*

(To audience/Vanessa:)

Before we close, I'd like to ask my standard questions. I'm going to say some words and you say what pops into your head.

HOST: Breakfast . . .

VANESSA: Chorizo.

HOST: Dirty . . .

VANESSA: Sanchez.

HOST: Rusty . . .

VANESSA: Trombone.

HOST: Donkey . . .

VANESSA: Thursday.

HOST: If you were a tree?

VANESSA: I'd be a hardwood.

HOST: Favorite word . . .

VANESSA: Cut.

HOST: Favorite toy . . .

VANESSA: Dildo.

HOST: Favorite *child's* toy . . .

VANESSA: Blow up doll.

HOST: No, a *normal child's toy.*

VANESSA: Pogo stick.

HOST: Here's one for Fernando. Fernando? What profession other than porn would you do?

FERNANDO: Life coach.

HOST: Least favorite word Fernando?

FERNANDO: Positive.

HOST: Finally Vanessa, turn ons?

VANESSA: Puerto Ricans.

HOST: Turn offs?

VANESSA: Puerto Ricans.

HOST: Do I have a chance with you at all?

VANESSA: No.

HOST: Thank you. And this concludes our show *Inside the Porn Actor's Studio.* Fernando . . .

FERNANDO: For pay? Sure.

(Smiles, poses and rubs his penis.)

HOST: This is so wrong.

(LIGHTS OUT.)

GO DIEGO GO

(Lights up. An excited female voice introduces our next character over theme music. A drunk, child impersonator dressed as the character DIEGO from the popular children's cartoon Go Diego Go *stumbles onto the stage. He rolls around on stage for a bit before he begins.)*

DIEGO: *(To audience:)*

Hey, is this little Jessica's Party? Hi, I'm Diego; Dora's cousin. I'm not the one from Birthday Party USA. I'm the one from Pico Rivera's Discount Party Personnel. We are *barato* and fun. So, where's the birthday girl?

(Sings while grinding his pelvis like a male stripper.)

Go Diego go! Go Diego go.

(To an audience member:)

Hey, don't cry little girl. I'm the real Diego. I'm just not animated like the cartoon, which means you can touch me. But if you do touch me remember: I can't touch you back. It's a legal thing.

(To general audience:)

Seems like the court's got a thing called a restraining order against me because they believed this little lying 15-year-old girl that looked 18. I met her during her *quinceañera*. Who would have known? So if any of you kids choke on a milk dud and you want me to give you mouth to mouth, you would die. I ain't ever going to be caught with my lips on some kid. You can't explain that picture away in the courts. I've tried.

(To an audience member:)

Now, back to the birthday girl.

(Sings while grinding his pelvis like a male stripper.)

Go Diego go! Go Diego go.

(To general audience:)

Oh, I got an announcement to make. Any single mothers at this party, for $50 dollars extra, I can stay after and go Diego go all night long. I can rescue animals, and I can rescue you from a bad marriage. You know what I'm saying?

(Sings while grinding his pelvis like a male stripper.)

Go Diego go! Go Diego go.

I want to set the record straight. I get pissed off the way they portray me in cartoon land. First of all, I look like a *puto!* Running around with a man sack rescuing animals! I'm Latino! We don't rescue animals, we eat them! I rescue a pig and it's going to be *carnitas* for dinner. And chorizo for breakfast because we save the leftovers.

Look, I'm the real deal. Because I got a cousin named Dora and she's an explorer. But that's just another word for "dropout." She got pregnant and she's got issues. Yeah, she walked out of school just like that movie *Walkout.* Which reminds me—I had an aunt that walked out of school and kept walking—no one made a movie about her! Hollywood constantly steals our stories and I'm sick of it. See kids, that's why Diego drinks—that and my failed acting career. I auditioned for the movie *Quinceañera* 16 times. But I refused to put out!!!

Hey! Let's see what's in my rescue pack?

(Pulls out a condom and rips it open.)

It's a balloon trick!

(Blows up the condom as if it were a balloon.) Now, Diego always wears this because if I don't, I'd be making a spin off. Little Diego and my big adventure would be finding child support. And I couldn't rescue that kid from a deadbeat dad. *(Regards the condom.)*

Look, it's a poodle!

(Throws the condom away and reaches into his backpack pulling out a map.)

Ah, Diego's magic map. This map tells when the Border Patrol changes shifts near the Arizona border, where Diego sometimes works with another animal called a *"coyote."*

Hey, who put a rattle snake in my pants? *(Reaching into his pocket)* Oh, that's my cell phone. *(Checks his phone)* Oh, shit it's Diego's rescue helper. My little bitch calling about when Diego's coming home. She'd like to collar Diego and put a homing device on me.

(A pregnant female dressed as DORA, holding a stuffed monkey marches out onto the stage.)

DORA: *¿Qué tú estás haciendo? ¿Porqué no estas en la casa conmigo? Yo estoy embarazada, ¡carajo!* When are you coming home?

DIEGO: *(To Dora:)*

I'll be home when I'll be home.

DORA: When?

DIEGO: I'll be home when I'll be home.

DORA: When?

DIEGO: I'll be home when I'll be home.

DORA: When?

DIEGO: I'll be home when I'll be home.

DORA: When?

DIEGO: I'll be home when I'll be home.

DORA: When?

DIEGO: I'll be home when I'll be home.

DORA: Fine!

(DORA marches off stage.)

DIEGO: *(To audience:)*

She don't trust Diego. Not since he got caught me with that pink power ranger impersonator, La Shanda. Ummmm, I love La Shanda. I love it when she uses her Power Ranger's transformation kit. It's amazing. One margarita and she magically transforms into a whore!

(To an audience member:)

Oh, I see you got a piñata. That's great.

(To general audience:)

A piñata is a good game to have for little kids. Blind fold a kid, turn them around in circles with other little kids around and let them swing wildly at a piñata. Great move. Why don't you give a kid a chainsaw!

(To an imaginary parent at the party:)

Hey, get your hands off me.

(To audience:)

Well, I hope you are having a great birthday Jimmy. Or Jessica . . . whatever the hell your name is. But I need to be more educational. So here is a real lesson for you: don't play with any Teletubby impersonators—especially the one with the purse. Don't trust that *vato*. Oh, and if you do go to school, stay in it! Don't end up like me, Diego. Running around to kid parties doing these gigs for money. I hate my life . . .

(To an imaginary parent at the party:)

Hey, man don't touch me! Wait, don't call the cops. I got a warrant.

(To audience:)

Look, I know that I'm not the best Diego impersonator; or that I'm not a good role model. But I'm trying, okay? I have a family and two kids, and another that I don't acknowledge as my kid—but he sure as hell looks a lot like me. The point is, I'm trying. You'll never see me begging for a handout. Because we don't do that. You'll never see a homeless Latino begging for money. We beg for jobs. Because we work. We want to make an honest living. So what do you say? Will you have Go Diego go down on you? It's only 50 bucks! Hey!!! Frigid women. Don't call the cops, I got warrants I'm issuing.

(LIGHTS OUT.)

THE PHARMACIST'S MONOLOGUE: PART 2

(BENNY "EL FLACO," the drug lord from Latinologues, *walks on stage. He is a very intense character with a "Wanted" sign on a screen that is behind him.)*

BENNY: *(To audience:)*

OK, say I make you a deal. Let me save you billions by giving you advice—stop the war on drugs. You are spending billions on a losing war because the only way you can win this war is to manage it and control it, like a budget. Because you will spend billions on this war and you will go bankrupt.

OK. We want to stop the war on drugs, but what do we do? But what do we do? We can't just do anything. We need to do something. And I say you are going to do something, and here it is . . . The only way that you can win this war is by not fighting the Narcos, but becoming one. You need to be the biggest one and control it all! You can control the damn like a faucet. Only *after* you control it. And the only way a Narco will listen to you is when he *fears* you. Now, you need the Narco man to think you are one of them or bigger than them. There is no easy way to shut off a river, but why not start diverting a river, controlling a river and eventually damming a river? Your hand will be on that spigot.

First, find a big Narco—and that would be me. I'm ready to serve this country. You give that Narco—that would be me—you give him some guns, extra killers and a few free lanes into the United States to sell it

WANTED BY FBI

BENNY "EL FLACO"

Narco Trafficking	Organ Trafficking	Sex Trafficking
Money Laundering	Sex Crimes	Parking Tickets
Murder	Child Support	MTA Violations
Human Trafficking	Loitering	Public Nudity

and let him—that would be me again—to become the biggest Narco that controls it all. And I mean it, MOTHER FUCKING ALL!

And what do you, the Government of the United States, get back? You get it all. Oh, we make a secret treaty between us. I reduce drugs into the United States. I reduce it by 20 percent each year. After four years there are no drugs coming into the United States. It's zero. Then I go legit. Now you got a political friend down south. Now it's political. I win for President and you get no drugs in the United States. I get a Narco dealership then you get less crime. I give my thugs who work for me plenty of drugs, poison them like rats, let them fight for nickels, get them to kill themselves and then we, the bad guys lose. I kill all the competition without the pesky slow courts. I clean it all up my way. Who better to stop drugs but a drug dealer? And the drug lords that turn legit and me—we are making real money in real jobs. The world is a better place. And then we all become rich, baby. We will control Mexico, but we will be legitimate like Sean Puffy Combs. You, the USA—are rich in control. Me, I'm rich in money . . . And you are the government so you can print some more money. Now just do the math. You spend very little money and get what you always wanted. But with me you get control. I work for you and you pay me by giving me Mexico—because you already have half of it already. I learned this from you America. Because you are the biggest gangster of them all.

(LIGHTS OUT.)

SLOW GUY

(A man stands center stage at full attention in a military uniform. This is SLOW GUY, and he's a bit . . . well . . . Slow. He's an ex-cholo.)

SLOW GUY: *(To audience:)*

Excuse me kids, glad to be here at my old high school to speak on the war. I'm not a recruiter. I'm just a vet back from the war. The first wave on any battle will always be Latinos, blacks and a few gay guys—it's a statistic. America wants to give us the chance to die for America. God bless America.

Many of you may remember me as a student here named Slow Guy. Yeah, they call me Slow Guy, they call me Slow Guy, they call me Slow Guy. I could never figure out why they called me Slow Guy . . . I went to this very same high school for almost two years. Good times. I learned a lot of education in auto shop—skills that helped me to see the Army as my only opportunity for me. *(He raps) I was running in the street up to no good in my hood with my hoody over my hood looking so good that the bitches even got morning' wood.* That's my rap. I learned to rap in Iraq. I was in a convoy guarding the USO tour with some rappers and comedians from amateur night at the Apollo—they went to Iraq to relax. Being heckled at the Apollo is a hell of a lot more dangerous than Iraq.

People ask me, "Slow Guy, what was the hardest thing about Iraq?" Well, I'd say, "Is that the voice in my head talking to me or a real person asking?" Then I'd answer, "Well, it was tough for me because every Iraqi looked like me. Look at Saddam Hussein, you put a big belt on that fucker, a big hat, have him dance *banda* and give him a beer and he looks like my Uncle Chuy from Zacatecas." War was hard for me because I'd see all these dark angry motherfuckers and I thought I was at a Raiders game when the beer runs out. It was tough on me on an emotional level because I'd get homesick. Or I'd be in the streets and some crazy *vatos* would roll up on us. They be mad dogging us then out of nowhere they'd start shooting at me. It would make me homesick for Compton. You never feel like an American until someone shoots at you. I never felt I was an American 'til they started shooting at me.

Now a lot of you kids are wondering, "Hey, I'm not as talented or educated as Slow Guy." Right? *(Beat)* OK. None of you, that's cool . . . Some of you are thinking, "How can I join the Army? I don't even have a green card. I'm not even a citizen for real." Well there is hope. The Army does not recriminate, imitate . . . discriminate. You fucking join, homes. Was George Washington a citizen when he joined the Army? OK, maybe he was. Well . . . but was Zorro a citizen when he fought in the Civil War? I saw the movie . . . I should've taken some history classes here. Well, I got a green card. I'm not a citizen. My family crossed here when I was small enough to fit in the glove compartment of their car. But when I joined I thought, "Here's my chance to get my citizenship." That's why I joined. Also my high school counselor and parole officer recommended I join the Army and serve in the war. And I said, "They'd never take me." But they said I was wrong, "The Army loves Latinos." For real. And that I'd do great in Iraq because I got a sense of the street. There were helicopters in the air, random gun shots, dark people all around that want to kill you. It was like summer nights in Compton.

The Army gives us Latinos a chance to be all that we can be. I became an army of one many times mostly because I got lost on patrol. I thought I could never qualify, but the Army said I was wrong. Yes, can you believe that? I got in. I even got in, in spite of my criminal record, lack of education and that drug test failure. The Army said I qualified for forward infantry or a scout or for medical experiments. I said, "Take me, Army recruiter. I seen action. How many recruits can do a field dressing and shoot a gun and do gang signs at the same time? I'm coordinated." So they put me in right away. They sent me to Iraq and I fought, and it was easy. I had a good sense of the street. And it don't matter where the hood is, it's all the same. All the same. I even saw people fighting themselves. The Shiite hit the fan with the Sunnies and it was on . . . I'd see them fight and could not tell the difference between them. Then I thought *that was me back in the day.* I mean, why did I fight anyone for rental property?

I fought with no education and only a green card to protect me. I got a better chance for becoming a citizen. I'm not an American citizen, but I fought for America. I was fighting for a country that doesn't want me. In a country that doesn't want me because my original country did not want me. That's fucked up in any language.

They used to call me Slow Guy in the hood. But I don't use my gang name no more. Violence and the streets is behind me now. I joined the Army. They should've named me Pinocchio because I got a leg made of wood. *(Lifts his leg and hits it.)* Well my dick's still good. That's the most important thing. They give you good medical attention if you're a vet. But they messed up my prescription for acid reflux. They mixed it with Viagra—my throat got hard and my penis burned . . . I'm in the fast lane to get my citizenship. So I'm doing good. I stepped on an IMP, a DUI, an MTV . . . Well, whatever it was, it blew me the fuck up. And that was that. So now that you know me, I hope you don't mind me speaking to you all. At first some pacifists refused to have me speak here but then they met me and they encouraged it . . . Stupid. But don't listen to them pacifists. No pacifist has ever won a war. Where was I? I hope this helped you decide to join. *(He salutes.)*

Private Slow Guy reporting for duty sir. I hope you do, too. And you guys in drama class, they got "Don't Ask, Don't Tell" so you can join too . . .

Hey, kids you got fish sticks today.

(LIGHTS OUT.)

Photo by Alan Mercer

Jacob Vargas as Slow Guy in Latinologues *at the Ricardo Montalban Theatre in Los Angeles. (2004)*

MECHA MADNESS

(Stage opens to the sounds of chanting. We see THREE MECHA MEMBERS—MECHA 1, MECHA 2 and MECHA 3—on stage. The leader and the two surrounding their leader.)

MECHA 1: *¡Qué viva la Raza, Que Viva la Raza . . . !*

MECHA 2: *¡Qué Viva la Raza!*

MECHA 1: *¡Qué Viva la Raza!*

I'm Quetzal Quatal Whitliococli Zolchilmilcho Gomez, and I'm the leader of this *Moviemento Estudiante* MEChA organization. Now, I'm angry but I'm not confused. I was created by the rape of our indigenous mothers and our Spanish forefathers. Death to Julio Iglesias.

ALL: And Enrique, fuck you.

MECHA 1: I'll be conducting this seminar in English.

MECHA 3: ENGLISH!

MECHA 2: Because he don't speak Spanish too good.

MECHA 1: I got a "C" in Spanish but that stands for . . .

ALL: CHICANO!

MECHA 1: Now I'm going to ask you some questions . . .

MECHA 3: *¡PREGUNTAS!*

MECHA 1: I'm going to say some words . . .

114

MECHA 3: *¡PALABRAS!*

MECHA 1: *¿Cuchi frito? ¿Plátano?* Don't mean nothing, okay? Menudo, soup or . . .

ALL: Group?

MECHA 1: Ricky Martin gay or . . .

ALL: Really gay.

MECHA 1: Good. I was just checking to see if you were really Chicanos and not some undercover Cubans or Puerto Ricans taking over. Cubans got their own promised land . . .

ALL: Miami.

MECHA 1: Puerto Ricans got their own island . . .

ALL: Manhattan.

MECHA 3: Puerto Ricans got two flags up. Humboldt Park. Two flags.

MECHA 2: All we got is one flag, Juan Gabriel.

MECHA 1: Flag fool. Flag.

MECHA 2: Oh, my bad. My bad.

MECHA 1: And a Puerto Rican guy stole my girl at Excalibur on salsa night. He was dancing fast and he was all skinny. He looked like Marc Anthony on crack. *(Sings Marc Anthony's 1999 hit "I Need To Know.")* "I need to know," shit, "I need to know." You need to eat motherfucker.

MECHA 2: Oh, look what we got here, homes, sitting right there. He's right in the audience. Look at him.

(They point to a nicely dressed man in the audience.)

MECHA 1: Oh no. Look what we got here. We got a beaner with a beamer. Look at you dressed all nice. Yeah, you all happy, you dressed all "IBM." You should be dressed . . .

ALL: I be MEXICAN.

Photo by Alan Mercer

Rick L. Najera and Paul Saucido in MEChA Madness *at the Coronet Theatre in Los Angeles. (2003)*

MECHA 1: Oh not too successful good. But if you are making money you will give it to *La Raza*. Good, I was checking. *La Raza* may call on you to drive me to school one day 'cause I got a DUI at Lalos during Cinco de Mayo. Now, we have had some scandals . . .

ALL: Scandals

MECHA 3: *El* Scandals.

MECHA 1: Because we were ambitious. Like the time we tried to change the name of Michigan Avenue to . . .

ALL: Michoacán Avenue. Ambitious

MECHA 1: Or the time we used fat people for our hunger strike. We got no sympathy.

(Points to an audience member)

He lost only five pounds in eight months. He cheated. Or the time we lost the money to our dance.

MECHA 2: *El Bailar.*

MECHA 1: Oh it was a great dance. Just the three of us. We danced slow.

(Sings Heatwave's "Always and Forever.")

"Always and forever . . . "

ALL: "Each moment with you . . . "

MECHA 2: Yeah, I got laid.

MECHA 3: Yeah, I got laid too.

MECHA 1: Yeah, I had a three way.

(Beat, realizing.)

ALL: We did it for *La Raza!*

MECHA 1: I dream of a day when we will be pure Chicano and a great leader like me will not have to live at home. But until that day, we will be holding a car wash. Anyone got car soap?

(Re: females in audience.)

Let's put those girls on the soap committee.

(Sings Sir Mix-a-lot's "Put 'Em on the Glass")

"Put 'em on the glass baby. Great. I like you people. You are all part of my oppressed minority group, and I'm happy to say that we are the smallest and most oppressed minority group on campus. So keep up the good work.

ALL: *Qué Viva La Raza. Qué Viva la Raza. ¡Qué Viva La Raza!*

(LIGHTS OUT.)

MY FATHER'S COAT

INTRODUCTION

I wrote this monologue after I lost my father. It later found a home in my one-man show, *Diary of a Dad Man,* which appeared on my *Showtime* special.

—Rick L. Najera

MY FATHER'S COAT

(Lights up. A man walks to center stage holding a long old-fashioned trench coat.)

MAN: *(To audience:)*

I love this coat. I love this coat. My father gave me this coat. When I was 8 years old my father gave me a coat just like this one. It was a long trench coat just like this one. I was so proud of that coat. I wore it to school and my best friend at the time was an Anglo kid named Nicky Whit. At school they called him "nitwit" for short. Teachers can be so cruel at that age. He said to me, "Hey where'd you get the dress? Where'd you get the dress?" I could never wear that coat again. I dragged it home and my father saw me and said "Hey what happened? *Mijo,* why aren't you wearing that coat?" I told him that, "Nicky Whit said 'where'd you get the dress?'" He understood. I never wore that coat again.

My father used to love telling that story. He would imitate me walking so broken and depressed at 7. He used to laugh telling that story. My father was a great man in my eyes. He spoke two languages. I speak one and a half. He fought in two wars. I fight traffic. He was a great man. He raised a family and had the same job for 30 years. I wonder if I'll have one job for over six months. My mother was a great woman in my eyes too. But somehow, it's our fathers that we, as men, compare ourselves to. Recently—before my father passed away—he gave me this coat *(refers to the coat he holds)* and said, "Hey _____, does it get cold in L.A.? Well, you should take this coat." I realized at that moment, that I had walked with giants. He raised a family, kept a job, did such extraordinary great things and made it look easy—almost effortless. I never saw him complain. He was selfless. And I wonder if I'll do half the things he did.

One time I went to Tijuana, Mexico, with Nicky Whit and he saw some kids begging for change. He saw people living in cardboard boxes, hungry and he said, "Hey _____, we're American. You'll never see that in America." Well, he was wrong. What to you expect from a kid named Nit Whit? *(Beat)*

I have seen things: people dying of diseases invented in my own lifetime and new deadlier diseases to come; terrorism in America and around the world; people getting poorer, hungrier—even in America; Enron; British petroleum; Afghanistan; Pakistan; recession; oppression, depression and Hollywood over obsession. Look at where we are. I have seen families living in cardboard shacks in America. Not Mexico. I have seen recession, bank closures, Wall Street implosion, deep-water oil spills, disasters natural and man made. I have seen things . . . And I wonder do I have the strength to change the things I see? What would he do? He was my hero and that hero is gone. I wonder, where will I find another? Was my father born with better genes than me? I wonder that maybe after years of fast food, Twinkies, McDonalds and ozone depletion, global warming terrorism, somehow we have grown weaker—and that our genes and sprits are weaker too. Not just me but all of us. I don't know . . . I don't have answers tonight, only questions. But I wear this coat and think, *yeah dad, it does get cold in L.A. Thank you.*

(LIGHTS FADE OUT SLOWLY.)

THE FAT MATADOR

PLAYWRIGHT'S NOTES

Of the many cast members who have played this, my favorites were Gabriel Iglesias and Momo Rodriguez. Each brought a funny and poignant touch to this role.

—Rick L. Najera

Graphics by Momo Rodriguez

THE FAT MATADOR

(A large fellow in black tights and a garment bag and matador hat walks onto the stage.)

I am sorry, I am sorry I am late but the bakery did not open till 10 a.m.! I love their bear claws, delicious. Thank you for seeing me, and meeting me backstage here in this arena.

I hear you are an amazing lawyer. I am a big fan of your commercials 222-2222 sounds like a train! Very catchy!

OK! I am a professional matador, perhaps you heard of me? No? I am facing discrimination and I need representation. I believe I have a legal case. They are harassing me at work, I don't mean sexual, believe me I tried. Look what they did to my suit! (He pulls a child's suit out of a garment bag). It's definitely smaller. Just before the end of the season and they are trying to get rid of me. I know it! I use to be the best. But lately, well the past ten years, I've had some trouble, mostly back trouble. They want to hire skinny matadors with no qualifications. It's this quota system, it's affirmative action. They have skinny matadors and forget better-qualified fat, metrically challenged matadors. They say I am metrically challenged about 100 kilos. They said I need to run with the bulls of Pamplona three times before I ever fight again. It's this quota system! They have to hire so many skinny matadors and plus-size matadors like me just don't stand a chance! I am triple XXX excellent! I defy the rule "one size fits all." Never sit in the front row in a comedy club, because I know better, I am not overweight, I am passed it! Way passed it.

I am not that fat, it's these bulls! These bulls are just too damn fast! What have they been feeding them lately? My God, these bulls are sponsored by Nike and have more steroids than Manny Ramirez! I feel like Elvis Presley during the Vegas years, but I said to my coach, he used to pack them in to an arena and so can I. But how do they expect me to pack into this suit? Look I am not fat! I am stocky, I have big bones, and I have an allergic reaction to donuts! They swell my belly up. Was Oprah Winfrey less worthwhile when she was fat? Was Michael Moore less a director? Was Shamu less a whale? No! Stop the insanity! I know they want to fire me! You have to help me. I know the signs; they mock me, they no longer send fried foods to my dressing room. The other day someone sent me some Jenny Craig Paella light. That was that bulimic matador from Bolivia. That's got to be harassment. Sue the skinny bastards! I can take a hint. Why all the celery sticks in my dressing room? I'm fine. I can still do my job. Except for the little stroke and high blood pressure and lower back pain. And the fact that I haven't seen my penis and shoes in about five years! Are they matching? Not my shoes! My balls!

These bulls are improving, why can't I! I am packing. Godamit I have a gun! Little Debbie Cakes and the NRA now sponsor me. I don't care if people boo me. Screw them, I am a modern bullfighter and plus everybody is doing it, P. Diddy, Lil' Wayne, Kat Williams, the Raiders! And it makes it so much easier to fight! (Break yourself Bull! Bang! Bang! Bang! Barcelona bitches!!) Oh hell with it. I am too nervous! I need food, some Hagen Daas ice cream and paella! And some good ham and Andalusia salami and a Diet Coke. (*Take a whiff of inhaler.*) I want to be a vegetarian but I like BBQ so much! And pie and Cheetos, well maybe I can loose a little weight, maybe I can have two shakes and a sensible nine-course meal and maybe buy a juicer! Yes! I can juice! I can juice bacon and cinnamon roll smoothies in the morning! Oh hell with that—I got rights! I am not changing. I got seniority. I know I have a case! I have a case of Cheetos in my car. I am sooo hungry!! I am telling you, it's not my fault! These bulls are just too damn fast!! They can't fire me! They can't fire me!

(HE EXITS THE STAGE.)

Right: Rick L. Najera (c.) and his lovely wife, Susie Albin-Najera, are joined by show producer Kevin Benson in front of the tour bus.

Left: Rick L. Najera (l.) and actor/ producer Rafael Agustín (r.) discuss production issues before a show.

Right: Rick L. Najera (second from right) and his wife, Susie Albin-Najera (r.) are joined by fans at the Imagen Awards.

Left: Cheech Marin (c.), who directed Latinologues *on Boradway, poses for a publicity shot with cast members (l.–r.) Rene Lavan, Rick L. Najera, Eugenio Derbez and Shirley A. Rumierk.*

Photo by Susie Albin-Najera

Left (l. to r.): Rick L. Najera, Academy award-winning actor Forest Whitaker and cast member/producer Fernando Carrillo following a performance at the Coronet Theatre in Los Angeles. (2002)

Photo by Susie Albin-Najera

Above: Eugenio Derbez (l.) and producer Robin Tate (c.) celebrate a successful show while on tour with cast and crew.

Photo by Susie Albin-Najera

Above: Tori Spelling (r.) is one of the many Hollywood A-list celebrities who have enjoyed Latinologues. Here she poses with cast member Paul Saucido.

Photo by Susie Albin-Najera

Above: Geraldo Rivera (second from l.) poses with B.D. Wong (second from r.) with cast members from Latinologues on Broadway. (2005).

Left: The tour bus for Latinologues racked up the miles on its national tour.

Photo by Susie Albin-Najera

125

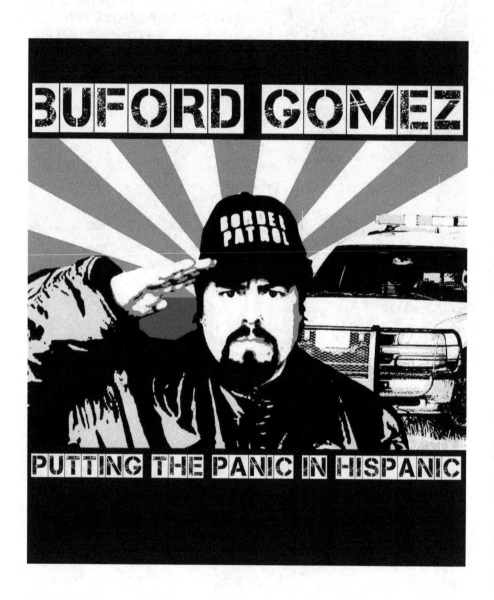

BUFORD GOMEZ

PLAYWRIGHT'S NOTES

This show can be performed by one or more actors. As a solo show, the actor performs all of the roles. As a multi-actor show, the actors divide the roles. Both male and female actors should not be restricted by gender, only by interpretation. Throughout the play, unless otherwise stated, the characters are addressing the audience.

This show is the end of a trilogy of plays. *The Pain of the Macho* was first performed at the Goodman Theater in Chicago and introduced its audience to Buford Gomez. *Latinologues* introduced The Manic Hispanic character and simultaneously reprised Buford Gomez. This play, originally titled *Virgins, Whores, Long Suffering Barrio Mothers and the Men Who Made Them* was later changed to *Biford Gomex* and ends the trilogy where it all started, at the border. This play was performed at the Alley Theater in Houston.

—Rick L. Najera

BUFORD GOMEZ

(A soft light goes up as a slide of a large American flag is projected on a screen. The stage is filled with this image as a man walks center stage sporting a large Mickey Mouse hat and holding a balloon. He is a U.S. Border Patrol Officer. His name is BUFORD GOMEZ. He looks about, his face obscured by dark sunglasses. A second actor stands next to him. This is JOSE—an over zealous Mexican trustee. BUFORD speaks with a very heavy Tex-Mex accent.)

(Each time a character or actor becomes a character, there is a slight adjustment of the light or sound or movement in the staging. The actor is required to change his world. The play is fast paced. Part monologue with a plot, it was my experiment in giving these characters a story.)

BUFORD GOMEZ: Well, well, well, look what we got here. Welcome. I have some fun tickets for a few families here tonight. The names of the people that I'm going to call out have won some exciting gifts. Great! I know you all are excited. Some of you have received a special letter in the mail. Can I see those people first? Is there a Ramirez family here, or a Garcia family? Anyone here by the name of Mohammed? Yes? Oh I see you. Is that your wife or daughter? I can't tell her age with that veil on her face. Is there a Mustafa Achmeddd—I may not be pronouncing this right—*(over-annunciating)* Mustafaaaaaaaaaa, Achaaaaaaaamed here? Very good. Is there a Sanchez, or Vargas, or Rodriguez family here? Well, all you people have won a free trip to Disneyland. Now, are you all ready to see the magic kingdom? Great. The big green tour bus outside is getting ready to roll so I'll just have to ask you people to get on aboard. Oh, "it's a small world after all," but as soon as you get on the bus it'll be a little less smaller. It's adventure land for you all. So get on moving people. Fantasyland awaits you all.

(SFX: People moving towards a door. A bus starting. BUFORD looks around, serious.)

BUFORD GOMEZ: There you go. Get on now.

(He takes off his Mickey Mouse hat and puts on a Border Patrol hat.)

BUFORD GOMEZ: Now allow me to introduce myself to the rest of you people still here. I'm Special Border Patrol Agent, Buford Gomez. What you all have witnessed is an INS sting. It won't be the magic kingdom they'll be seeing; it'll be the tragic kingdom. They won't be seeing the electrical parade lights; they'll be seeing the border stadium lights. They're going to the real never, never land. Because they will never, ever return. That may seem cruel to some of you, but we are serious about immigration. Now, there is a right way to come to this country and a wrong way, and they chose the wrong way so they got to hit the highway. We're not cruel at the Border Patrol. I love children; some of my favorite raids are on day care centers. I love kids. I make sure the bus will pass by Disneyland and we will have some happy meals and some Disneyland sing-a-longs on that bus—a real family deportation vacation. Some are actually saving money and earning frequent deportation miles. It's a chance to reconnect with their families.

(He puts on a Border Patrol jacket. JOSE walks into the audience grabbing a member of the crowd.)

JOSE: Get on the bus. On your feet convict. Get on that bus.

BUFORD GOMEZ: *(to Jose:)*

Hold on Jose. That one's okay. He's legal.

JOSE: *(to Buford:)*

You sure? Okay, I'm just trying to help.

BUFORD GOMEZ: That's Jose, a trustee. He's staying in this country to testify at a smuggler's trial.

JOSE: The black guy did it! It was the black guy.

BUFORD GOMEZ: Not now Jose, at the trial. I'm Officer Buford Gomez and welcome to this seminar on the United States Border Patrol.

JOSE: Say hello to him. Say, hello Officer Gomez. Say hello Officer Gomez. Say it! He had a hard night.

BUFORD GOMEZ: I had a rough one. It was an Oscar de la Hoya fight and that border was jumping with people crossing. Worse than that, a Julio Cesar Chavez fight. I'm Mexican-American. I was born in El Paso in the great state of Texas in the United States. I'm a Mexican-American; some might call me more American than Mexican. Well, I said, "Who asked you, you liberal hippie. It's cavity search time, you "Willie Nelson look-a-like." I'm proud to be a member of the Border Patrol. I hope you all will be too. There are lots of Mexican-Americans working at the Border Patrol. There's donuts in the back and coffee for later. I even got some nice *pan dulce*. So let's get started. I'm here to answer your questions on the Border Patrol and explain what we do. This may be a recruitment seminar on the United States Border Patrol; but I consider it a chance for you to learn why I love my job. I love what I do. Deportation is my business and business is good. I'm happy to wear the green. Many of you are here tonight to decide if you have what it takes to join our men and women of the United States Border Patrol. Well, we will just have to find out, won't we?

Some of you may be here from Neighborhood Watch, some of you are from the organization Light up the Barrier—they shine their car lights onto the border, sometimes the Mexicans shine mirrors back at them and they have light wars. I see the head of Light up the Barrier, Mr. Greg Barnes, here tonight. Thanks for the support. Some of you that are here are concerned Latinos and tan people that may have been stopped numerous times by the Border Patrol and are worried about your rights. Some of you may be criminals trying to learn trade secrets. Whoever you are, sit back and learn. People, that was a sting. I consider that not a bad sting. It was more of an, "Ouch!" But that sting is just one of the ways we keep the cultural roar in this country to a minimum. That's a "sting." You will learn all sorts of techniques by the United States Border Patrol that keep America, American. If you join us, you will learn to be a lean green deporting machine.

(The projected photo on the screen changes to an INS photo.)

BUFORD GOMEZ: Now, we have got all sorts of ways to catch illegal aliens; stings are my favorite. Stings work. One of my favorite ones was one we did in San Diego. It was called "Meet the *Baywatch* Girls."

JOSE: *¿Donde? ¿Donde?*

BUFORD GOMEZ: Jose, just listen. It was a Meet the *Baywatch* Girls and Los Tigres del Norte at a *carne asada* barbecue sponsored by Tecate Beer. Now, that was a big hit. *(Beat)* Let's get started. Let's do a *grito* to warm up. Wow, lots of Latinos tonight. That's good. Now if you want to truly become a Border Patrol Officer like yours truly, you need to understand who you're catching. We at the Border Patrol study fascinating cultures so we can best capture them and deport them. We at the Border Patrol have to watch over 5,000 miles of border; prison guards are pussies. What do they watch? Maybe a few hundred inmates? We are watching billions AND they are coming, people, to this great country whether we like it or not. Lady Liberty has got her legs spread and there is only us between her and a big illegal gang bang.

(JOSE mimes having sex with Lady Liberty.)

JOSE: Say my name! Say my name!

BUFORD GOMEZ: There are already six to 12 million illegals in the United States—four to five million are Mexican. Up in Naco, Arizona, we caught over 60,000 in over six months. It should be called Nacho Arizona. There are 80,000 people legally crossing into this country each day; we are here to protect our border. There is a silent invasion happening and there has not been a single shot fired. Well, who's going to stop this illegal gangbang of Lady Liberty? Who? Me! And hopefully, some of you. Why are so many people crossing? Well, some say nature hates a vacuum; that life always wants to fill up a vacuum. Now, I agree, because what is happening at the border sucks, but I will stop the tide. Why? Because I love this country. I fought in Grenada. I fought in Desert Storm. I fought in Panama. A Gomez has fought in World War II, I, we even lost a Gomez at the Alamo. He was the first recorded incident of friendly fire in this country; he was killed by Davie Crockett himself. I guess Davie didn't realize there were plenty of Mexicans fighting for Texas in the Alamo. Now a re-enactment, "Hey, you Mexicans out there are really going to lose. Gringos always win. Why you looking nervous, Mr. Crockett? What do you mean Señor Crockett? You saying no one's coming for us? What do you mean we're out of . . . ? Hey, Santa Ana, these fucking gringos kidnapped me." I had another cousin killed by friendly fire in Panama because he was short with acne and a Marine sniper mistook him for General Noriega. So it was an honest mistake. Last year we lost a Gomez fighting with the Marines, it was at a bar in Bakersfield and he was dating a Marine sergeant's wife. Well, he found out, and words were exchanged, and well . . . Point is, is that we are fighting men—us Gomez's—and we love America. America loves to give us minorities the chance to fight and die for this country. Mexicans are always in the first wave of any war. There are more medals of honor won by Mexican-Americans than any other minority group. In the first wave of any Battle you will find a Mexican-American! They should've made *Saving Private Martinez* instead of *Saving Private Ryan* except it's mathematically impossible to kill off all of any Mexican family's brothers. You won't see Mexicans in movies about the war. Hollywood forgets us but luckily the Army doesn't.

Well, we love this country. I first got interested in immigration back in Texas in El Paso on the border—that's where I was born. I used to get arrested so many times in those INS raids as a child. I got interested in the Border Patrol during my frequent questioning by the Border Patrol. I used to get arrested because I had a terrible stutter so I couldn't say U.S. Citizen. They'd say "Citizenship" and I'd say yyyyyyyyooooooooouuu. I'd start stuttering and wouldn't stop 'til they brought me to the border. One time they sent me across the border. I said youuuuuumother fucker I'm American—I had a bad stutter. Well, I got to meet so many of the Border Patrol guys that they kind of adopted me. Some kids collect playing cards I collect Border Patrol statistics. I've been thinking about marketing some collecting cards. Like Buford Gomez—number one in arrests. I'd be holding my baton pointing to where I was going to send you. I'd be M.V.P.—Most Valuable Patrolman. I'd be Daryl Strawberry without the hookers and the crack. I'm good at what I do. How did I get so good? I got so good by studying my opponent.

(*A slide comes up on the screen. It says "Mexican History."*)

BUFORD GOMEZ: To understand how to catch your illegal alien you better know their history.

(*A slide comes up of the map of Mexico. Slides are used minimally to give the illusion of a seminar. Only key slides are used to demonstrate certain points.*)

BUFORD GOMEZ: Mexican history started really when Cortez landed in Mexico. Most Indians were happy to see him, they thought.

JOSE: Look, tourists.

BUFORD GOMEZ: That's right. You see folks, at that time Mexico was just populated by savage Indians known as Aztecs. They believed in virgin sacrifices. Mexico had lots of virgin sacrifices. But there were not as many virgin sacrifices in Puerto Rico or Cuba. I believe Puerto Rico and Cuba did not have virgin sacrifices, because virgins are so rare in those islands. They drink piña coladas and it's hard to remain a virgin with a piña colada in one hand and a Puerto Rican Ricky Martin in another. And for a woman, it's even harder. Well, Cortez encountered the Aztecs killing virgins so he rescued a young virgin girl named Malinche. He rescued her by taking away her virginity as quickly as he could. She was Cortez's interpreter and girlfriend. The Spaniards then decided that these savages needed religion so they converted them to Catholicism and helped them find God. Some savages did not believe in their God so Cortez killed them so they could meet God in person. After the Spaniards came to Mexico, Mexico became the number one exporter of gold and spices and slaves in the world at a time when there really wasn't much export business at all. The Spaniards brought full employment to Mexico and Catholicism and the Aztecs became extinct—although many Mexicans have Aztec and Spanish blood in them. They're called *mestizos*. But I think a more accurate term is Spaztec. That's Spanish and Aztec blended together. I think Spanish and Aztec or the Spaztec race is far more accurate.

JOSE: Buford is Spaztec.

BUFORD GOMEZ: I'm of the Spaztec race myself. The Cubans blended Spanish and Africans together to create . . . Celia Cruz—also known as the afro-cubano race. In Cuba, they got Chinese-Cubans called "chinocubanos-africanos." But I just call 'em chinks with rhythm. There is nothing stranger than seeing a Chinese-Cuban cussing in Spanish.

(Imitating a Cuban-Chinese man speaking Spanish.)

Coño, Coño! I say call a young priest and an old priest, it's freaky.

Remember Latinos come in every size, shape and color; and it's mostly large size because they love to eat the fried foods and barbecue. Don't be

133

fooled, people. We come in every size and shape and in most everybody. Latinos have penetrated most every country. Latinos are, right now, doing some penetrating somewhere in the world—mostly in East Los Angeles or Chicago or New York. They're penetrating deeply, smoothly, then building to a climactic finish. Sometimes listening to some cool jams, "Always and Forever."

(JOSE does a slow dance and sings along. BUFORD stops. He shudders a little then composes himself.)

BUFORD GOMEZ: Yeah, we've been all over this great nation and through most people in this great nation. A lot of people in America have had a little Latino in them and a few car trunks have had lots of Latinos in them. My favorite thing to do is walk up to the trunk of a car, knock on it and say, *"¡Qué viva Mexico!"* No Mexican can resist that. *"¡Qué viva Mexico!"*

JOSE: *¡Qué viva!*

BUFORD GOMEZ: *Qué viva,* Mexico.

JOSE: *¡Qué viva!*

BUFORD GOMEZ: Mexicans invented all sorts of things, such as carpooling. We know how to fill a van, let me tell you! A cousin of mine invented the double-decker van during a *quinceañera.* We also invented the concept of duality—the concept that things can be two things at once.

(JOSE demonstrates, holding each item out as BUFORD speaks.)

BUFORD GOMEZ: Like swim trunks can be underwear or swim trunks, it can be a trash bag or a suitcase; it can be a garage or a family room, or both. Duality. We invented theories on time relativity, if your relatives are visiting, it just seems like time stands still. Another law of time, relativity—time relativity is that no relative will leave unless they have to pay rent.

Now for some facts . . . There are 45 million Latinos in the United States. Latinos are the second largest population in the United States. Los Angeles has the most Mexicans and New York the most Puerto Ricans. There are also an estimated six to 12 million illegal aliens in the United States today, and most of them are Mexicans. So there are even more

Rick L. Najera as Buford in Buford Gomez.

Photo by Alan Mercer

Mexicans here than are showing up in the census reports. Listen, if you doubt me go to a flea market or a swap meet in your neighborhood and you'll say, "Damn, where did all these Mexicans come from?" The United States is the fifth-largest Hispanic country in the world. Who do you thinks' buying them bad Ricky Martin records? Not white kids in Kansas, they're buying bad rap albums. Los Angeles is over 54 percent Latino at one time.

JOSE: We used to be a 100 percent.

BUFORD GOMEZ: Jose! Back to history . . . After the Spanish made all them Spaztecs, Mexico declared its independence, left Spain and stopped being a Spanish colony. They then became a French colony but the Mexicans kicked out the French on Cinco de Mayo because they thought it would make a great drinking holiday. Then in 1849, the United States invaded Mexico and was brutally attacked by the Mexicans—and it took the Americans a long time to get those Mexicans to brutally attack them. The Americans had to shell and shoot at the Mexicans and invade Mexico before they could force the Mexican army to brutally attack them; but once they did, we declared war on Mexico. Now a lot of people in congress were against the war. In fact, Abraham Lincoln was a Republican Congressman opposed to the Mexican-American war. He even lost his next election because he was considered a traitor for not supporting the war. Even the Irish soldiers refused to fight the Mexicans. About 200 actually deserted the American Army and joined the Mexican Army. They were called the San Patricios. Even most artists were against the war. Writer Henry David Thoreau said, "This war is wrong. If we swallow up Mexican land it will be like a poison pill." Lincoln, the Irish, Henry David Thoreau all were against the war and boy, were those losers wrong. President Polk wanted the war and he knew we could win. That's the history of our southern neighbor.

As for our northern neighbor, Canada . . . God, I hate Canadians—those pasty bastards stealing hockey jobs from good old American boys. Well their history is hum . . . They really don't have any history. How can you record history when you're freezing in an igloo? Your hands are shaking too much. Canada is America light basically—all the land with half the culture. Canada is a frozen wasteland and they're not our real concern. The Canadians that come here are normally just television stars, Jim Carey amd Michael J. Fox.

We will concern ourselves with our southern neighbors. Oh, of note, before I forget, Puerto Ricans are legal. I repeat. Puerto Ricans are legal. Yeah, they are born U.S. Citizens—but there is no harm in collecting names and addresses for them just in case.

JOSE: Why are they born legal? It's not right, we're closer. Who'd Maria from *West Side Story* screw to get that deal?

BUFORD GOMEZ: Yeah, I know it's not fair. Don't get me wrong, Puerto Rican people are good people. I love Puerto Rican women . . . but they are crazy. In fact, most Latino women are crazy. I know Anglos like to call 'em "spitfires" or "hot tamales," "firecrackers," "Latin bomb shells." But these are just words for "fricking nuts." I had a Puerto Rican girlfriend once who practiced Santeria. She loved Santería—that's a kind of Latino Voodoo or magic. You see, your Mexican women will basically cook a chicken, but a Caribbean Latina will sacrifice it. I don't mean to generalize folks. But believe me people, if you generalize it will make being on the Border Patrol that much easier. Let's do some generalizations: Cubans are Mexicans on rafts and Puerto Ricans are just legal Mexicans. Not all Colombians are selling drugs. Some are actually taking them. Argentineans are not all Europeans but all Argentineans *think* they are European. Peruvians are just Japanese-Mexicans. *Folklórico* dancers are all gay. That's a generalization and a fact. . . . That's enough generalizations for now. Back to Puerto Ricans. I had one Puerto Rican girlfriend and she would yell out, "*¡Ay papi, ay papi!*" I told her, "Is there something you need to talk to me about?" It was weird. One time she did some Santeria on me when I couldn't get my missile to rise—must've been stress from work. It was during Christmas and that border was hopping; hopping fences, running with presents in their hands. Last time I was that stressed was during that Elian Gonzales incident. I knew that kid was a set up. He was called Elian like *illegal alien.* Tell me Castro didn't plan that. But after she sacrificed that chicken I was as good as new. Only thing was, I couldn't make love to her unless she was covered in feathers. She came home one time and caught me cheating on her with my down comforter. That's a little Border Patrol joke. Here's another. Knock, knock?

(Audience response:) Who's there?

BUFORD: On.

(Audience response:) On, who?

BUFORD: On the floor motherfucker, that's who. No one ever gets that.

Oh, we have fun in the field, it's not always serious. One time we hooked a car battery up to that chain link fence at the border at night—it was Macarena time all night long! But it isn't always fun. We have to carry weapons. It's dangerous but we got a new thing, we got a pepper-ball shooting gun. I once seasoned my barbecue with it. I love my job. I got a good job, a great wife. Mexican women come in two types—good girls and really good girls. My wife was a good girl, not a really good girl— although, after a couple of beers she can turn into a really good girl. She wants kids and my night shift has been a form of birth control. She says her biological clock is ticking but I say put on the snooze alarm and shut up and let me sleep. I have been trained to stop Mexicans, not create them. It's hard to teach an old dog new tricks. I love her, but I do not want kids.

(A slide of a picture of an attractive Latina.)

BUFORD GOMEZ: She's a great woman—she tamed the animal in me. Don't get me wrong, I'm still a lean, mean, INS deporting machine.

JOSE: He's the man who puts the "panic in Hispanic."

BUFORD GOMEZ: Yep, I'm the man who puts the "baton to Juan." I put the "pepper spray on Jose."

JOSE: He put the pepper spray to me. He'll put the "mace in your face." He's the "best at the arrest." He puts the Bill of Rights to the test . . .

BUFORD GOMEZ: Okay Jose.

JOSE: He puts the "ill in illegal."

BUFORD GOMEZ: All right! Inez and I've been married about three years. She's a great woman. She wants to have a baby. Why do I want to help a baby come in? Hell, there're 45 million of us here. We are doing all right, legal Latinos are thriving; my job is tough enough. There are illegal Mexicans trying to come here 24/7. There are lots of aliens coming here. They're coming folks, and they are smart. They're tricky. I found one illegal, had an INS jacket on walking backward across the border, it almost worked. But he slipped and fell down. Another time I saw some illegals dressed as highway workers picking up trash along the highway. Their disguise was real good and it almost worked, but I noticed they were sweating. No County worker ever sweats. That brings me to my next point . . . to be a great Border Patrol Agent you must have various skills and aptitudes. At the Border Patrol we have a program called DEPORT that stands for . . .

(Jose writes on a chalkboard upstage. D . . . Delivering; E . . . Illegal; P . . . People; O . . . Out of here; R . . . Rapidly; T . . . Today.)

BUFORD GOMEZ: D . . . Delivering; E . . . Illegal; P . . . People; O . . . Out of here; R . . . Rapidly; T . . . Today. That stands for "Deport." Repeat if you will, let's all say it. DEPORT!

JOSE: Is illegal spelled that way? I took English and that's not right.

BUFORD GOMEZ: I know that illegal is spelled with an "I" Jose. But we need a catchy slogan, so work with me people! Look, we have a problem people. According to statistics, any person coming to the United States has a one in ten chance of having a Ph.D. Whereas a U.S.-born person has a one in one thousand chance. I know what you're thinking we got some smart people trying to come here, how we keep 'em out? Exactly!

It won't be easy! Then you got the problem of the traditional Mexican that believes that California, New Mexico, Texas, Arizona and parts of Colorado are their traditional homeland.

JOSE: It's my traditional migration route. I need the Sierra Club to protect my ass; I'm the endangered species! Fuck the grey whale. I'm as cute as a baby fur seal and even more needy. Look at my sad eyes.

BUFORD GOMEZ: That's it. You want to wait in the van?

JOSE: Air conditioning on or off?

BUFORD GOMEZ: Off.

JOSE: I'll be good.

BUFORD GOMEZ: They are coming on over to work their traditional area. The Aztecs traded as far as Colorado, as far as Oregon, native people have been traveling all over this land for thousands of years. So it's a hard habit for them to break. That's why we have a steel or Iron Curtain that we have erected at the border. Now East Germans put up their Iron Curtain to keep their people from leaving but we put up our Iron Curtain to keep people from living; from living here. It's frustrating because Mexico won't stop them from coming. If they did, their economy would suffer. Mexicans are sending money back to Mexico—it's their second-biggest economy. Their first is tourism and third is petroleum. Their economy would suffer a $6-billion-dollar-a-year loss. Then again, so would our economy. Mexico is our second-largest trading partner. Of course a stable Mexico serves the United States. But there is a right way and a wrong way to immigrate and strapped to a radiator is definitely the wrong way. Where was I? Immigration has always been a problem. Why actually, the biggest immigration happened not now but in the 1800's– 1891 through about 1901. People really started noticing immigration when people got darker—Italians, Sicilians, Arabs—most of Hollywood's future Jewish directors and writers came to this great nation then, and the Irish. The French were so happy to get rid of those people that they gave us the Lady Liberty statue. Now the plaque on it says, "Give us your poor, your huddled masses." But we at the bureau want to get it amended to read something simpler like, "Don't land" or "Keep moving." We could have the statue made to look like this. Jose . . .

(JOSE poses . . . First as "Lady Liberty" pushing people away, then as a woman flipping someone off, and then other various poses.)

BUFORD GOMEZ: It would show the real new spirit of immigration in this country. We not only have to deal with assuring no one gets here, we got to deal with the drug lords on the border. The Tijuana Cartel controls all the border. They are controlling drugs and illegal immigrants. The head of the Tijuana Cartel has a $2-million-dollar reward on his head and no one can find him. I guess people figure, *why get a $2-million-dollar reward if you will never live long enough to enjoy it.* This job is dangerous—drug lords, illegal aliens, *coyotes*, and Jeeps that flip over. People that throw rocks at us—and Latinos are good baseball players so you know some of them got a good throwing arm. Only night clerks and pizza deliverymen have it more dangerous than us. Still that TV show *Cops* won't do a TV special on us. Come on. Well it just pisses me off. I even took some acting lessons just in case. *America's Most Wanted* don't want us either. It's just plain prejudice. I did a ride along with some Hollywood producer. Boy, was he a real *folklórico* dancer type. He wanted to do a series about us. I never even got a return phone call, nothing. It's the border. You're going to get ratings. The Mexicans will tune in to see which cousins are getting busted and employers will tune into to see who's coming in on Monday and who's not.

(Buford's cell phone rings offstage. JOSE runs offstage and back onstage with the phone in his hand.)

JOSE: It's for you.

BUFORD GOMEZ: *(To audience:)* Hold on.

(Into phone:)

Hello? Baby, I'm doing my Border Patrol seminar. I'll be home soon. Look, don't call me while I'm working. What if I had been undercover? You could blow "Huggy Bear's" cover. "Huggy Bear" . . . That's my undercover name, "Huggy Bear." It is not a stupid name. Well if I had been undercover, my cover's blown now. Don't put my Mom on. I'm on damn . . . Hola! Si mama, ya me voy a la casa muy temprano. Menudo, ay que sabroso. Con Jello? Que rico! Si, mama te quiero. Good bye.

(To audience:)

Sorry about that. But, you know women, they worry. Our jobs are tough on the little ladies. They're always worried. -- I wear a bulletproof vest and a lead jock strap in case I get radiated at one of our checkpoints. -- It's the families that suffer. They go through some tough times when their loved ones are serving on the border patrol, but they support us. My mother is proud of me. My father passed on. He died in a trucking accident; he was listening to Enya when he fell asleep at the wheel. They heard Enya playing in the background on the black box.

(He gets choked up.)

I'm sorry. I'm Okay. My mother is very supportive of my work, she even volunteers. She does citizen patrol on Sundays at the airport in San Diego. She was stopped so many times, she got curious about Citizen Patrol. She found out what these people did and decided to join. She loves meeting international passengers and questioning them—she's a communicator. The world is getting mobile and so should we. There are new scams thought up every day to come here. Cultural evolution is what we're doing here. We are ensuring the strongest, fastest illegals get here. As for me? I'm proud to say I'm not evolving. Why? Because I'm perfect like the cockroach.

JOSE: He's perfection. Buford is like a big cockroach.

BUFORD GOMEZ: Thank you Jose. The cockroach has not evolved in a million years. I'm perfect. I will never evolve. I'm like a big cockroach. Any questions?

JOSE: That *guero* (light) looking guy's got a question Buford.

(Lights change slightly along with the character change.)

RICK: *(V.O.)* Yes. I grew up in San Diego about 15 miles from the border. I'm your typical Mexican-American. I grew up in La Mesa, Barrio La Mesa. I'm Mexican-American and I want to know . . . Why am I always stopped? It really angers me. First off, my father fought in Vietnam. My brother was in Vietnam. Two of my cousins fought in Vietnam. Two of my uncles served in Korea. My uncle died in World War II, in the Philippines. Yes. He was on the American side. My mother is Mexican-American as well. I know I'm light. I'm *guero*—that's Spanish for good looking, tall, Mexican man—but, I get stopped by the Border Patrol. Listen my point is . . . Well, she's from Iowa, yes, Boon, Iowa. There are lots of Mexicans there. Well they were on the train going to Texas. Her family fell asleep, they missed their stop and they woke up in Iowa. I grew up on mid-western cooking—ham, string beans and corn on the cob all wrapped together in a flour tortilla. I'm a *guero*, but I'm Mexican-American. But more importantly, I'm a U.S. citizen. I mean, I'm an American. My family has paid their dues but I'm getting stopped by the Border Patrol. A lot of Latinos are. In Arizona, two out of three Latinos have been questioned or stopped by the Border Patrol. Its like, "Do you have your papers please?" I feel like I'm in one of those World War II movies.

(German accent) "Your papers? Your papers, please."

I have been stopped at the San Clemente border check point, at the El Centro check point; these are all a 100 miles into the United States. I've been stopped on Amtrak trains. Come on! I'm not wearing *huaraches*; I'm just wearing regular clothes. The point is, is the Border Patrol racial profiling? That's my question.

JOSE: Buford, we got a radical here. Buford, we got a real troublemaker. You got a problem? That's not a question that's sediment. He's making sediments. He's not asking questions. You're ignorant.

(Lights change again revealing BUFORD thinking and listening tentatively.)

BUFORD GOMEZ: That's "statements" Jose, not "sediments." Wow, sounds like there's some anger there son. Now let me get this straight. You are not wearing obvious Mexican clothes, right? You have no *"Qué viva Mexico"* sticker on your car? You have no "I 'heart' Puerto Vallarta" sticker your car? Is your car low to the ground? Are you eating a *chimichanga* and listening to Los Tigres Del Norte?

JOSE: Is there nachos or tacos in your car? Sometimes a car may smell of chorizo.

BUFORD GOMEZ: I'll handle this radical Jose.

JOSE: I'm going to get some pepper spray.

(JOSE exits.)

BUFORD GOMEZ: Do you have an older relative? Maybe a grandmother in braids, a grandfather wearing a *vaquero* outfit? You know, with those big hats. Maybe he has a moustache wearing a big hat? No? Wow, and you're still being stopped by the Border Patrol. Well, the answer is you're just unlucky. Yep, that's the answer. You are just unlucky. Must be some sort of karmic debt. I read about Eastern religions. I deported some Buddhist once we got to talking. That must be the answer because there is no racial profiling. Now sit down and let's get on with this seminar. I got a lot to cover.

Let's describe a typical day in my life. I'm a field agent. I work in the field. There are house agents—they work in the house with the master . . . That's not coming out right. I'm a field agent. Let's go to the field. Jose, Jose . . .

(SFX: A car starting.)

BUFORD GOMEZ: That's strange. Sounds like my van. Oh, damn it. Jose, get out of there! That's government property! . . . damn it.

(BUFORD runs off stage, then runs back on to center stage.)

BUFORD GOMEZ: Hold on, just talk among yourselves. I'm going to have to hit myself on the head and say he overpowered me. Damn it!

(Lights go off. We hear a dog barking. Buford's wife INEZ enters. She is an attractive Latina.)

INEZ: Why is George W. barking? Is there some trouble boy? Is Buford in trouble?

(Buford's mother is heard off stage.)

MOTHER GOMEZ: He's a dog, he's not Lassie. Come on grow up! Hey where's the TV changer? Inez.

INEZ: Come on boy . . . *(To: Mother Gomez)* He seems really upset. Maybe something is wrong.

MOTHER GOMEZ: Yeah, ask him about some lucky lotto numbers.

INEZ: Come on boy. I'll get you something to eat.

(Dog stops barking.)

INEZ: Maybe he was just hungry.

(The lights dim. INEZ walks off stage. We hear Tijuana norteño *music. It sounds like a circus. The lights begin to flash/swirl—similar to disco lighting. Stage left is a wanted poster for BENNY that is found at the border. The poster reads "Reward: $2 Million Dollars." Benny—a conflicted insomniac and frustrated stand-up comedian with an ironic sense of humor—walks center stage.)*

BENNY: That's me. I'm worth $2 million dollars, I'm a worth $2 million. I could call them up, turn myself in and collect the reward and then escape. I have thought about it. Yes, I have. But it would cost me too much in time lost. I used to send these "Wanted" posters out as Christmas cards. People really laughed. I wish they would catch me.

I have never had a vacation, truly never. Don't feel sorry for me. I knew what kind of business I got into. I'm not like one of those whiney child stars that say they had no life. "I had no life!" "Oh, poor me!" People say Michael Jackson had no childhood. I say *fuck him.* I know kids working in sweat shops in Tijuana. Now they've had no childhood. Sweat shop kids would love to have a father like Joe Jackson beating and forcing them to sing. At least that would be some sort of attention. Those poor kids don't have a life. Feel sorry for them, not Michael Jackson. And don't feel sorry for me. I don't have a life either, but I knew my responsibilities.

I'm a good man, really. Sure, I killed a bishop in Guadalajara, but that was a mistake. I even asked for papal forgiveness and that don't come cheap. Believe me. You see he was at the airport in the same kind of car that a rival drove and well, these hit men of mine are not exactly well-oiled precision machines. They were nervous. Sure they get nervous like anyone else—it's not like the movies. You try shooting into a crowded airport. You don't know how many bodyguards they got . . . You're scared. I'm not a killer like them but I'm human, I can imagine how they felt. I'm in management, I'm more white-collar, but they were scared. They are blue-collar workers. I truly felt for them. I felt bad killing them, really, but it's a matter of discipline you know. There is no hit man school, no hit man college; maybe there should be but until there is, more innocent people will die.

Maybe the NRA could have gun schools in the United States. It would help stop those drive-by shootings you read about everyday. They always shoot everyone but the gang member. Old women, kids, babies get shot but never the gang member and the gang member is wearing bright colors! Still they can't hit them. And most gang bangers, these guys can't really run very fast. They are great targets you know. You drive up and they're holding a 40-ounce and kicking it with their "homies." Like they say, they're not ready to run. You think they would be easy targets. They're wearing baggy clothing too; but they always shoot some innocent bystander. The NRA could help them learn to shoot better.

The point is killing is not as easy as people think. It's ironic. Teenagers that should not have babies get pregnant by looking at each other, but 40-year-old professional couples can't get pregnant no matter what they do. They would make great parents, but some crack-addicted teenager has no problem getting pregnant. It's ironic. All her crack boyfriend has to do is to look at her and she's got quintuplets. Professional killers can't seem to kill the right person. It's hard for them to successfully kill the right people. But some nut, some postal employee ends up killing 13 people easy. It's ironic that some kids in Colorado can kill lots of other kids easy and they're not professional killers. They can even make pipe bombs—I don't know how to make a pipe bomb. I'm a fucking criminal, and I don't even know how to make a pipe bomb. It's ironic. This world is crazy. The world is full of ironies. It really gets you thinking. Not even the CIA can kill Castro, and that's the CIA.

You see killing is not easy. So why do I want to kill this border patrolman? This agent? This Buford Gomez? Well, I really don't, but the lower management thinks it's a good "signal" to the U.S. government and that it will "send" a message. A message, like I'm some kind of political person. But I'm not really a *político*. I'm not. I know politicians; they're greedy—greedy for fame, greedy for money. I'm not greedy. It's just business and it's a very good business.

I'm in it because of demand. But it's very competitive. You can't make mistakes. I don't want to kill this man. He's an American so it would really show we're so-called real "bad ass" guys. Like I'm some sort of Robin Hood, a Zapatista type. But then again Emiliano Zapata only killed the armies of a dictatorship. Killing an American? Well, not even the Palestinians have done that. Americans are valuable. It's a value thing really. Like when Jews are killed it's news, but when Palestinians are killed no one cares. Why? Because Jews are more valuable—because they're rarer. I have thought this through.

I used to stay up at night a lot watching CNN because I had a cocaine problem. Ironic, no? Of course it was not a real problem because I have no problem getting it here. *(Pulls out a bag of cocaine.)* See, I got 200 more tons of this stuff. I don't have a problem getting it. So I was not a real drug addict. I was like a Starbucks employee who just drank too much coffee. A Starbucks employee can have as much free coffee as he wants, but it just keeps him up at night. It was the same with me. I can have as much cocaine as I want. But it just keeps me up at night. So I thought about a lot of things. I played lots of Yahtzee. I was going to write a book but no time, plus I'm a horrible typist and most secretaries would be terrified of working for me. I thought about kidnapping a writer, Tom Clancy, but I just got sidetracked; I have no concentration. I get distracted.

Where was I? I have I have attention deaf . . . I have attention defi.. def.. def . . . deficit . . . Look apples! That's a joke! I used to love watching *Evening at the Improv*, I saw them use that joke four times in one night. I always wanted to go to a taping of that show and heckle. I can heckle good.

Where was I? Oh yes, killing this American Border Patrol Agent. It's something to think about. Killing him, I look strong with my people but I lose by taking on America. Return him? I look good or I look weak. If I keep him, I look good but I also look like a terrorist. Americans hate terrorists. Drug lords they can live with, but political thinking people? Fanatics? They are dangerous. What if I wound him? Cut off a hand? Release him and pay him for his pain and suffering? Eeny, meeny, miny, mo catch a . . . I know, I'm going to see what's on TV.

(Lights go back on BENNY.)

BENNY: I wonder if WWF smack down is on? Or MTV's Real World?

(The lights begin to change. BUFORD GOMEZ stands center stage. He looks around.)

BUFORD GOMEZ: Lights on the border are blinding lights.

Photo by Alan Mercer

Rick L. Najera in *Buford Gomez.*

BUFORD GOMEZ: Okay, this is the field. It's tough. We patrol the hills in our vans. Across there is Mexico—Wild Mexico, Old Mexico, land of my ancestors. But I'm legal, they're illegal, that's what separates us. That and lots of iron fence. I was born here. I'm an American citizen. American citizen is the greatest words one can ever say especially when you are crossing the border. When someone is crossing the border, first thing we ask is, "Where were you born?" or "Your citizenship?" That simple question is what separates most people. The Romans were proud to be Romans; citizenship was everything to them. Citizenship, most people take for granted. It's another thing that keeps us apart—the wire, the roads, the desert, and the ocean.

San Diego is a barrier town—it's surrounded by borders. A border in El Centro, a border before you get to the outside, an ocean to the west, desert to the east, borders everywhere. I just deal with one border, sometimes two. I work the San Clemente border, mostly the Mexican border, but sometimes we patrol as far inland as Los Angeles. I'm working in the fields. Not only do we catch aliens, we catch drug shipments. I had a dog—George W. He would've taken a bullet for me and when I held up like this he saved my life. He took a bullet for me. He's on medical leave; he was a great partner, he loved me.

Sometimes we find bandits in the field. They wait for the *pollos*—that's what they call people trying to cross. They rob the men; rape the women . . . real scum. It's really bad. We have so many people here causing crimes you don't know who to bust. You have to decide who's more important: drug runners, robbers, or illegal aliens.

When I'm in the field it's peaceful, aside from the stadium lights and screams, helicopters and running, screaming people. But there are moments when it's quiet. It can be real quiet when you are out in the field. Where I patrol near the Tijuana/San Diego border, you can see the beach from your patrol car. There is nature. You can see nature in all its glory. There are dolphins playing in the surf, eagles flying overhead. *(Interrupts himself:)* Hey, look! An endangered spotted yellow Tern's nest. Right here on the ground. It's a perfect circle.

(BUFORD turns around and unzips his pants. We hear BUFORD peeing.)

BUFORD GOMEZ: Just like those bulls-eyes in those urinals. *(Sings)* "The Circle of Life!" Hey, that's weird the ground's almost opening up and oh LORD!!!!

(BLACK OUT.)

(Buford's wife, INEZ, enters. She stands center stage. She is the keel on Buford's storm tossed ship.)

INEZ: I've been waiting all night with no word. Damn him. I worry about him. He wears a bulletproof vest, but you never know. I pray to the Virgin. She has known suffering.

You know why we love the Virgin? Because she has suffered she knows suffering. We all love virgins. I remember when I was a virgin. It's tough to be a Latina; we have to be a wife, a mother and a virgin, and that's not easy. We have it hard. We are groomed to be married and be virgins. We have *quinceañeras*—sweet-15 parties—just to be one year ahead of those skinny *gringas*. The Aztecs needed virgin sacrifices. You know why? I believe because virgins were worth something. You know why? Because Latinas love sex and keeping our virginity is not easy. Latinas have to be virgins and mothers at the same time and that's not easy. That's the real sacrifice, staying pure. Our only sexual problem is that we have to act like we don't enjoy it—because we do. I love making love. I love being romantic. I know that's not politically correct.

Telenovelas are so popular and they're not real. But we still love them because they're fantasies. The maid gets the rich man in the *telenovelas* but not in Mexico. In Mexico the maid only get's fired. It's a fantasy. Ricky Martin, he's another fantasy. Juan Gabriel is gay. I'm almost sure of it. I'm going to go out on a limb here. But I think he is. But women throw panties and bras at him at his concerts . . . then again so do some men.

We love fantasy. I have a fantasy; I want to have a child, a baby. Latinas love our babies. I'm going to tell you a secret. Once we have our babies they become everything. They're our little *rey,* our *vida,* our lives. We love them. We don't have Oedipus syndrome, we have Eduardo syndrome. We spoil our children. The Mayan women spoiled their babies so much because they felt they were angels and they had to spoil them so they would not return to heaven. I want a child. Malinche wanted one. Malinche, I understand her. When Cortez came to Mexico, he was given a slave girl named Malinche. It means either from the sea or strife. Malinche was both. That's what love is. It's strife sometimes and all women are from the sea. We are constantly changing, and we cry salt tears and will drown you like a rat if you cheat on us. That last part I had to reach for. Well, Cortez could never have defeated the Aztecs without her. She was an Aztec. And she saved lots of Indians. The Spaniards would've killed them all. She saved as many Aztecs as she could. Her Aztec mother had sold her into slavery but she forgave them. She tried to negotiate peace. She was not some whore. She gave him two sons, one Don Martin, who was a favorite of Spanish King Ferdinand. She was the mother of all *mestizos.* She was not raped. Her home that Cortez gave her still stands in Mexico City. She built a home that she raised her sons in. She conquered a nation with Cortez. Her only crime was that she loved Cortez. She loved him.

Love. That's every woman's weakness and her strength. Well, I love my Buford. I know what he does. I know who he is. He's a Border Patrol Officer, he arrests people like me and him. He's trying to keep the peace. He does not dislike Mexicans, he just loves America. But this is his country and Mexico is his country too. You can love two countries. He just can't see that. But you can't forget your past. And a child between us, that's our future; Malinche realized that a child will never leave you, it will unite you. A child will always love you and will always be yours. Cortez left for Spain to look for more glory. He did not realize that he had all he needed in Malinche. That's his tragedy. I hope Buford realizes that I'm here waiting for him and if he doesn't that will be his tragedy too. He's been missing for a day. They don't know where he is. His damn dog keeps barking. He could be dead. I should've frozen his sperm and kept it in the freezer just in case. I could've kept it next to the frozen yogurt or our anniversary cake.

I want a baby. If we had a baby, I would always have Buford with me. But you know, I think the real reason women have a need for a baby is, because the man we love, well, we can never completely control him. But a child we can. He becomes our little man that we can totally control. *(Resolved.)* It's about total man control. Not procreation. I should not have said that. *(Sweetly.)* It's about total control and love. Please Virgin, bring Buford Home.

NEWS MAN: *(VO:)* The hunt continues for a missing Border Patrol Agent in San Diego today. The FBI has been called into the search but hopes are dimming. On a lighter note, the San Diego Zoo is looking forward to another panda.

(BUFORD walks on stage he is blindfolded and wearing handcuffs.)

BUFORD GOMEZ: *(To his captors:)* I think we should legalize drugs. I'm with you guys. I know that sounds liberal for a law enforcement officer and the fact I been captured by Narco traffickers and they have threatened to, I quote, *"cut my dick off and put it in my mouth and sew it shut"* end quote. Wow, do you guys have an imagination. I mean, would there be any anesthesia involved with that cutting of my dick procedure? No! Well, hell. I mean it's not like you guys can't get any drugs. Listen you all got me here but they'll be looking for me. Hey, come back here! Let me see your boss.

(Sounds of a door clanging shut. BUFORD unties his blindfold and looks around.)

BUFORD GOMEZ: Well, I really have got myself in a pickle here. These Narco traffickers don't realize they ain't playing with a strong hand. A Mexican-American Border Patrol man is a weak hand, a white FBI agent would've been better hand. Hell, a white woman with kids that's a straight flush. Hey, one of them Bush daughters would make a better hostage. A Bush daughter? Well now that's a royal flush. Hell, they could've lured one of 'em across the border with offers of free margaritas. Put some salt on the lip of the border, they'll come. It's almost spring break. They'll probably be here partying anyway. They would have been good bargaining chips, but not a Mexican-American hostage. Hell, they'll be lucky to get a return phone call.

Mexican-Americans are not good bargaining chips. We make tortilla chips. We ain't hostage bargaining chips. I love America but it's just economics. You got a plane load of American tourists and you got a plane load of Mexican-Americans, you tell me who's going to get the $3 million in unmarked bills and a helicopter faster? The Mexicans' barely get on those Spanish networks to report on it. Remember that plane load of Mexican-American hostages captured in Egypt? Well you probably never heard of it. I know you have never heard of it because they were not news. They were a little group of Mexican-Americans from La Puente visiting the Holy land. By the time it got on the news those Mexican Americans became Egyptian suicide bombers. But I saw the videotape. I saw the luggage they uncovered after the crash—it had duct tape on it, so you know they were Mexican. And there was no suntan lotion in their bags but lots of hotel shampoo bottles and towels from hotels from around the world, so you know they were Mexicans. Plus they had lots of little bottles of tequila in their bags. Mexicans love tequila. But here is the real giveaway that they were Mexican . . . they saved their airline food. They saved their airline food for later. Who would save airline food? Only a Mexican would do that.

I'm not paranoid. I'm enlightened, and if I was lighter instead of enlightened I'd be out of here. Some might say I'm only saying that we should legalize drugs to get in good with my captors. But we should legalize drugs. It would hurt the drug people most in their pocket books. If we gave Pfizer, Dow Chemical the rights to legally manufacture illegal drugs like cocaine and marijuana . . . If they could create drugs and market them, there would be old-fashioned competition and free market. Drug traffickers would be out of business. Madison Avenue could get involved. We would hear slogans like "Columbian cocaine, it's the richest kind" or "Buy American—try crystal methamphetamine." You'd see new products like the crack patch. You wear it and it reduces your craving. Or instead of Nicorette gum there would be Narcorette gum, made of pure heroin. It would make nicotine addicts look like pussies. They'd have slogans like "Try Narcorette—keeps you from throwing up and shaking." Our farmers in Kansas City would be in big companies cutting their 100 acres of marijuana followed by herds of hippies smoking the stubble. There would be celebrity endorsements, "Hi, I'm Robert Downey, Jr., and I'm here on a plane feeling no pain because on Continental, we offer free drugs in first class. The friendly skies just got friendlier. Who needs extra leg room when we got extra head room? Oh stewardess? Could I have a pillow? My face is melting. I see it all. Legalize drugs and we put criminals out of work and put drugs where they belong—with the pharmaceutical companies and with the alcohol and tobacco companies. Sure we might destroy Starbucks, but believe you me; fast food will get even faster. You'll have your food before you order it. You'll never have the munchies. Watch out Ronald McDonalds, they're coming to get their food. And imagine a new kind of happy meal complete with pipe and some crack. Legalize it, and maybe they will let me free. *(He struggles with his handcuffs.)*

Oh damn, these are on tight and they're my own handcuffs. There's an irony here, but I just can't see it. Oh God, I hope they let me go. If only I hadn't been walking around, if only I had stayed in my cruiser. But I had to go; I was peeing on a rare endangered tern's nest.

They got these rare endangered birds near my area. Well it's kind of a bull's eye thing to pass the time. Guys know what I mean. So I'm aiming and peeing on this tern's nest and . . . Well all of a sudden the ground gives way. I thought the earth was swallowing me up! Then I end up in the dark tunnel. I must've fallen about ten feet. And I look up—and God have mercy—I uncovered a little highway under the ground, a big tunnel. It was a tunnel for smuggling drugs or illegals or whatever right under my feet. I hit the mother load! I swear to God I saw a carpool lane on one side of the tunnel it was that big! I reach for my radio but it's in my car. Then I reach for my gun. Sure enough I see a bunch of guys coming up with assault rifles. Well, it pleased me to see the NRA was working. They had assault riffles and plenty of guns and they started shooting at me and they were good shots—must've been that NRA outreach in the barrio program. They were good. So I basically weighed my options. Then I surrendered like a man. I hope they don't try anything funny with me like . . . I don't know? Have their way with me? It's a curse to be good looking. They may take my body but they cannot take my spirit. These handcuffs are kind of erotic. Oh God, they're going to kill me. I have served my country well. They'll rescue me. Keep calm, Buford. I'm Buford Gomez.

I'm decorated; I got a perfect attendance medal that's got to count. Okay, forget it. I'll die defiant.

We should not legalize drugs. There is right and wrong, crossing borders illegally is wrong except in the case of East Germany. Oh damn, I'm sounding liberal. Drugs are wrong except in the case of pain killers. Then again, self-medication is what some people are doing. Prozac is just heroin light. I'm getting confused. Homosexuality is wrong except in the case of Siegfried and Roy. I saw their show, it was good! Gambling is wrong except in the case of Indian reservations; bingo is a traditional game among the tribes. But there is a right and wrong and holding me here is wrong. Let me go! I won't tell no one. I swear—unless I'm forced to testify. Why can't things be just black and white?

(Lights up on the MANIC HISPANIC. He is a very effeminate, schizophrenic, conflicted man; a Mexican Merv Griffin—and just as masculine. He's high in the Hollywood hills perched on the Hollywood sign.)

MANIC HISPANIC: (*To audience:*)

All right, I know this is not positive. I'm against violence and suicide is the ultimate violence. It's murdering yourself. I'm murdering my little inner Hispanic child. I'm up here on the Hollywood sign on the H for Hispanic. I know, *how cliché.*

I have to kill myself. It seems like the right thing to do, the Hollywood thing to do. I'm no longer with the studios. My films flopped. *Titanico—* Cubans on a raft with a slow leak—sank quicker than the *Titanic.* Who would have believed it? *Saving Private Martinez* couldn't save me. And Paul Rodriguez in *Montezuma's Revenge,* the comedy, didn't quite work even with the talking Taco Bell Chihuahua. It was an old Yeller kind of thing. That dog was on drugs or something. He humped my leg. The set was a nightmare. Even Paul Rodriguez humped my leg too. It was strange.

I was brave after being fired. Sure, I cried and handcuffed myself to my desk. All studio executives do that! But then I thought, *well when one door closes, another opens.* But a lot of doors were closing—the doors to my leased Mercedes, the doors to my summer cottage in Nantucket, the doors to my office, they were even locked. Then my roommate/slash secretary Enrique filed a sexual harassment suit against me. Well, I never!

I like girls. I do! Then things got really bad. You know there are triggering events in life that make you do these things. Mine was simple. I was at the market buying a mud mask, some Evian and some soy milk for my lattes, because I'm lactose intolerant. *Mia Culpa. Mia Culpa. Pardoname.* I live with the shame of lactose intolerance one day at a time. But I was saving money buying an at home do-it-yourself facial mask. I had really sunk low. Even when you're feeling suicidal you should look good. Well this gang-banger type, this *cholo* walks up to me and says, "Please sir, buy some candy so I can keep out of gangs." And then something snapped. I just said, "No." And he grabbed me and said, "Please sir, buy my candy so I can stay out of gangs." And I lost it. I said,

(*To gang-banger:*)

"I don't want you to stay out of a gang. I want you to stay in your gang. Stay in your gang! Because there's loyalty in a gang, not in my world. I'm not in a gang and look where I ended up, broke with nothing. So listen *cholo*, I'm not going to buy any candy from you because I want you to stay in your gang. Stay in your gang. There's loyalty in a gang. People care about you in your gang not in the corporate world, not here. You have loyalty in your gang. Your 'homey' your 'dog' your 'bro' your 'blood' would kill for you. He would die for you, sell crack on a street corner at 3 a.m. in a New York blizzard for you. That's loyalty! You tell me. Would some frat brother do that? Would your buddy in the Kiwanis Club do that? Would your golf pals do that? Hell no. So stay in your gang, there's loyalty in your gang. Stay in your gang, you will find faithfulness. You will learn hand/eye coordination—especially doing drive-bys. You'll be in shape—you're always running from someone. You will learn skills like acting. Hollywood loves to employ real gang members as extras. The Latino actor's life goes like this, 'Mom, I want to be in a gang' to 'Mom, I'm in a gang' to 'Son, I used to be in a gang.' Then finally, 'Come, here my grandson, I used to be in a gang, oh my heart, the chorizo.' So listen you *cholo*. You stay in your gang. You'll learn pride. You'll learn geography. They always know their hood. They never leave their hood. You'll learn self-defense, you'll learn about business in a gang. And it's a secure business. No business I know of will have customers offering to blow them for their product at three o'clock in the morning. Hell no! So stay in your gang. (*Angrily*) Your life will be more exciting, more terrifying, and a lot shorter than mine so stay in your gang. Because I'm not buying any of your damn candy!" (Beat)

(Back to audience:) Well, the *cholo* mugged me and stole my Gucci loafers and all my maxed-out credit cards. And then I really lost it. Then I ended up here. I mean, what's the point of it all? I was planning to kill myself, and then it happened. I looked around and I saw all the lights down below in Hollywood. They look like campfires; a thousand campfires huddled together scared of the nights, scared that the night is breeding beasts, hungry young uneducated beasts with nothing to lose. Then I realized that we're all scared. That's all, we're scared of the people around the fire and we're scared of the beast in the night surrounding us. Then it hit me up here. I finally knew who I was. I'm not a Latino or Hispanic or Mexican-American. I'm scared of what I really am and so is everyone else. And if a shallow Hollywood former studio executive like me could realize that, then maybe we're all going to be alright. We'll all be alright as long as we stay together. And maybe we'll even invite the beast in the night to join us around the campfire and feel the warmth of the fires, and better yet of us. And if we get together we might be less scared.

So I finally know who and what I really am. I'm scared, and I feel a lot better. So I'm coming down from here. God, what was I thinking? They really should have lit steps. If I fall I swear to God I'll sue the bastards. But then again if I die they'll think I committed suicide. Maybe I should write a un-suicide note. Okay now, I'm really getting scared. For real, I'm going to fall. Oh, damn if they find me dead they'll think it's a suicide. Now this really sucks. *(Whispering)* Help, help, help. Help! Maybe those gang guys down there stripping my car will hear me. Hey, help! *Cholos*, up here! *¡¡AYÚDAME!!*

(Lights down on the MANIC HISPANIC. Lights up on BUFORD in his chair. Off stage music is heard.)

BUFORD GOMEZ: I'll use my police whistle to get my dog, George W. I know he'll hear it and come to save me. That dog loves me. *(He pulls out a dog whistle from his front pocket and blows it.)* I hope that dog hears that.

God, last night I had a dream. I had a dream about my life. In it, I allow one illegal to come across the border. I let just one through. Do you know that story about the butterfly? It's like this, a man goes back in time but he steps on a butterfly, well then he goes back to the present time and everything has changed. It's a story by Ray Bradbury—or maybe I read it in *Hustler*. The point is, one person, one illegal could change everything if we let them through. I'm at the border, when you go to the border you notice it's chaos. There is a little revolving door that lets people to the Mexican side. It's like how I imagine hell, just a revolving door going only one way. And then there are all these fences and people waiting, illegal aliens. Then you see these large lights along the border and roads and just us patrolling. There are thousand of illegals in those hills and there are just a few of me's. I can hunt—I think because I'm Mexican-American. So my Mexican side knows what I'm thinking. My American side asks my Mexican side, "Are you planning to cross?" And my Mexican side says, "Sí. But don't tell no one, *paisano*." Well, my American side says, "Sure, no problem." Then my Mexican side turns to my American side and tells on the Mexican side. That's called a split personality, because I'm Mexican-American.

It's in other cultures, this split personality. African-Americans, Asian-Americans, Native Americans, each with two sides inside them at war. I have a black partner. His name is Jim Jackson—no relationship to Michael Jackson or Jessie Jackson or Reggie Jackson. Damn that's one talented family. Well, Jim? He doesn't have the same issues I do, but if he was in Florida he would. Why, there you got French-speaking brothers in inner tubes. If he was in a patrol car in Compton, he would have issues like me. What do you do when you're busting your cousins? You got to feel bad. Those are Haitians, they look like Jim, and these Mexicans look like me. Well if he had to bust them he might feel bad too, but I've been trained to get over any guilt I'm feeling. I remember I'm not busting my people. I'm busting illegal people. My supervisor Achmed said, "Damn it Buford, fuck you my friend you bust them illegals." So I even talked to my supervisor Wang Ho and he said, "Damn you Buford, you think I got time? You get them Irregaraows." He can't pronounce "L" sounds. So that's what I do.

But one time I was tracking in Arizona with some Indian Border Patrol Officers. -- Yeah, they're real good trackers. Indians make good trackers, I saw an Indian track some aliens in the dark. I said how did you do that, Tonto? And he said "Ancient wisdom and night vision goggles." He was good. I mean, Indians been here a long time and since all they have learned to do is hunt, track and deal cards. They get good at tracking. Indians have time to learn to be great trackers. -- Well we tracked these aliens in the desert and it was hot, broiling hot. You need about a gallon of water to survive each day in the desert. These coyotes drop off illegals and tell 'em to walk about an hour to the highway with maybe a quart of water each. But the highway is about 45 miles in the desert. They get lost or they turn "Quail"—that means they break into smaller groups.

The desert is unforgiving to anyone with no water. Funny but El Paso is running out of water. In 25 years Juarez, Mexico, will run out of water. Water is important, it's life. Water is power and these people in the desert got no water. They don't have no food, nothing. They start to lose it after about a day. People will drink their own urine and their kidneys get permanently damaged. They're getting sunstroke. Their water's been gone for a day and they start dropping all their belongings, and we're following them. We find them and we're tracking them and I see some baby clothes and diapers. Little baby shoes. Baby shoes. It tore me up. I was holding these baby's shoes in my hand and I lost it. We found those people—over 15 people—all over that desert. We never found the baby and mother 'til much later. They looked like mummies, that's how dried out they were. They looked just like mummies. We never identified them. They were buried in unmarked graves. I visited those graves and I put water on their graves on *El Dia de los Muertos*, a.k.a. Day of the Dead. That's an old Mexican ritual. I don't believe in Mexican customs because I'm legal. They're illegal and they're from the other side . . . but we are so alike. Ain't that strange?

Well, I don't want no kids. I told Inez no kids for me. I don't want to bring a baby into this world, not after seeing what happened to that baby. I don't want to see baby shoes or diapers or baby bottles. I'm doing my job. I don't know why I told you all that. But . . . maybe that baby would've come here and grown up to be a doctor that found the cure for cancer, maybe invented some great invention, maybe joined the Border Patrol. Maybe he would have ended up being president of his high school or had a son who became president of the United States. Kennedy was a son of an Irish immigrant. Why not a Mexican immigrant? It could happen. Well I wonder about that baby. I wonder about a lot of things. But I work nights so I can wonder a lot. Sometimes I come up with answers. Most of the time I don't.

(Lights down. The barking of a dog is heard. Lights up. INEZ walks on stage and finds MOTHER GOMEZ on her knees praying to the Virgin of Guadalupe wearing a black headdress. MOTHER GOMEZ loves to bet on

the dogs and horses in Tijuana, drink beer and smoke her Pal Malls. She speaks with a raspy voice and an accent.)

MOTHER GOMEZ: My sins have come back to haunt me. Buford is going to be killed. It's on the news. Oh my God.

INEZ: Just calm down. Tell me what's wrong. Have you been drinking again?

MOTHER GOMEZ: I have self-medicated with four margaritas. Damn it's working, I feel better. But it was appropriate. It's like cussing—you can only do that when it's appropriate. I heard that once. Like in the old days when no one cursed unless it was appropriate. Like in Custer's last stand when Custer cussed. He said, "Shit! Look at all the fucking Indians." That was appropriate. Or in Titanic the captain said, "Damn, this water's cold." That was appropriate or in Pearl Harbor the commander said, "Wow! Look at all the fucking Japanese." Well, Buford was kidnapped by the Tijuana Cartel.

INEZ: By the Tijuana Cartel?

MOTHER GOMEZ: Well, he is fucked. I'm not just cussing, what I'm saying is appropriate.

INEZ: Please Mother Gomez, calm down. Tell me what happened.

MOTHER GOMEZ: They got my boy. My little Buford, *mi vida, mi rey,* my king. *Mi corazón,* my heart. *Mi razón de vivir,* my reason to live. Pray with me, Inez. Pray with me that the Virgin will hunt them down and curse them and boil their eyes out if they hurt my boy.

INEZ: That doesn't sound like the Virgin. She's kind . . .

MOTHER GOMEZ: She's also a mother. Don't mess with a Mexican mother's baby. Even that Gloria down the street, she defended her boy. She said he was never in a gang. He was a *cholo* through and through. He spray-painted my front yard.

INEZ: That was address numbers on the curb to raise money for his high school.

MOTHER GOMEZ: He was raising money for his crack and I'm not talking about the one he was showing while he was spraying those numbers on the curb. They got Buford. He was captured as he was investigating them.

INEZ: What? That's impossible. They would've called me. You're just imagining you heard something. It was a dream.

MOTHER GOMEZ: My boy is just so brave. It's on the news. He was on patrol. Must have been surrounded by a 100 or more. They must've overpowered him before he could commit suicide. He would never be taken alive.

INEZ: Let me call the station. His captain will tell me what's going on.

MOTHER GOMEZ: Later. Not now. I have a confession and you must never tell anyone. Swear. *(She kneels and pulls INEZ down with her.)*

INEZ: Sure . . . But . . .

MOTHER GOMEZ: You cannot tell anyone. If Buford found out it would break his heart. He would tear out his eyes.

INEZ: Like Oedipus?

MOTHER GOMEZ: Who's Oedipus?

INEZ: The Greek.

MOTHER GOMEZ: I'm talking about Buford, you're talking about Greeks.

INEZ: He was a Greek king that married his mother and had sex with her.

MOTHER GOMEZ: Ay, I knew a Dominican who did the same thing. I saw it on Jerry Springer. It was his salute to Latinos on Cinco de Mayo. Listen to me. Never tell Buford what I'm about to tell you. Ay, my sins have been visited on my Buford. I had a horrible past. I'm no virgin I had sex with other men.

INEZ: While you were married?

MOTHER GOMEZ: No, I never cheated on my husband. I have morals.

INEZ: I'm sorry.

MOTHER GOMEZ: No, I had sex with other men when I was a prostitute in Juarez, but that's not the bad secret. Oh hell, I probably slept with as many men as those girls I watch on MTV spring break. Those *putas*? They're doing it for free. Shameless. Doing it for a free drink and some CD's. I was working. I was doing it for money. I was a professional sex worker.

INEZ: Look, you had to do what you had to do to escape poverty.

MOTHER GOMEZ: No, I wasn't that poor. I wanted some new clothes. That's all. I saw that all the girls in my village that dressed nice, came back from working as "secretaries" in Juarez. I knew that no secretary was going to make that kind of money. So I figured it out. I told my family that I was going to Juarez to work as a "secretary," even though I don't know how to type or do anything else. They had to believe it. They watched *telenovelas*. They figured the worst I could do was end up being a maid and marrying some rich man's son like Thalia did. Well, it was nice working in the bar "Adelitas de Juarez." They got these bars in every border town and I made lots of cash.

INEZ: I heard of those bars. You just have to be hostess and let guys buy you drinks? Right?

MOTHER GOMEZ: Yeah. That's it. But the real money is in screwing them. It was a hard thing to do. I just wasn't used to standing up for that long in heels. Well one day there was this Mexican who saved up all his money to come to the bar. He had been in El Paso working as a *vaquero*—a rancher—that night he was going to cross to work in America. He said there wasn't a border that could keep him in. His name was Conception Gomez and he was a big Mexican.

INEZ: How tall?

MOTHER GOMEZ: No, he was a big Mexican. Well he was tall too . . . and he looked just like Buford. I bet he is much older today but still good looking. Well he was going to cross again but he saw me and decided to stay a night and cross in the morning. I was fine looking then. Well he bought me drinks and we talked and he was handsome. Damn nice ass too. And we talked and it was romantic and we went upstairs to my room and, well, made love all night long. He sang me corridos. (*She sings "Y volver, volver."*)

. . . And we drank tequila off each others bodies and rubbed lime and salt on each other. Then he left. Then I had enough and I quit, but I was pregnant by him. A border couldn't keep Conception in and neither could a condom.

INEZ: The prostitution is your terrible secret?

MOTHER GOMEZ: Oh, big deal grow up. That's just sex. No, it gets worse. I had Buford in Mexico; we crossed illegally when he was one. He fit in a glove compartment of our coyote's car. Well I raised him in the United States with forged papers. Buford's back is wet.

INEZ: Buford is illegal? But what about Buford's father, the one that was killed in the trucking accident? The Gomez war hero?

MOTHER GOMEZ: I lied. I said he died asleep at the wheel after listening to some Enya. I told him I heard it on the black box they recovered from the truck. There's no black boxes in trucks. I married another Gomez who died a year later and made the rest up. It was all a lie. You know most history is a lie anyway. He wanted to believe what I told him.

INEZ: Really? But . . .

MOTHER GOMEZ: I told him to love America. After all, in Mexico there was no future, here there was. That's why I love it here. I love the United States. Any Mexican that's here is here because we were betrayed by Mexico. All that patriotism in Mexico is for the poor. It's to keep them in line. Believe me the rich in Mexico City are only patriotic about money, and they only like American presidents, not *pesos*. Most Mexican presidents have ripped off the poor for generations. There was no future for me there I was just smart enough to see it. Now you must never tell Buford. Let him believe his dreams, *mijita*. There, thanks for letting me get that off my head. I'm going to make another margarita and get some sleep. Well, now if you do tell Buford this secret I will destroy you Goddamnit . . . *(Beat)* even though I love you. Good night *mijita*.

(MOTHER GOMEZ walks off stage singing "Y volver, volver.")

INEZ: This is one truly messed up family.

(Lights down on INEZ. Lights up on the MANIC HISPANIC.)

(He is on his cell phone.)

MANIC HISPANIC: Listen, I need some credit. I need a little loan. I got a job. Yeah, it all worked out. I'm over that "we're all scared" crap. I'm more scared of unemployment. I got a deal all because I'm Latino. Yeah thank God it worked in my favor this time. They need me. I need to go to San Diego tonight. I just got a producing job . . . the same people who did *Selena* and the Elian Gonzales story and the Menendez brothers. Yeah they're good, they specialize in Latino tragedy so they're always working. Oh yeah, they're good. Their motto is, "If it cries, we buy it." It's their motto. Well, they think there's another Latino tragic story happening. Yes, it's another Latino tragedy. I missed out on *La Bamba* now I'm not going to miss out on this one and I better move quick because the only Latino stories Hollywood buys are tragic Latino stories. I wish Ricky Martin or Enrique Iglesias would get trapped in a well or something.

They want me to get the rights to the Buford Gomez story. I knew Buford Gomez. I was doing a ride along at the border and I met him. He's a Border Patrol Agent. He's totally conflicted. He's a redneck Mexican, seems he's a hero now. Well he was just captured by a drug dealer so it's conflict. I'll need my assistant and an office in San Diego. God, that town is boring. I can smell Sea World from over here. San Diego may be boring but only 15 miles away is an exciting story in Tijuana. They think I'm the perfect person to get the rights to his story because I'm Latino. I'm a Latino and it's a Latino story. Well maybe I might even see Buford. I know someone who might get me a chance to meet Buford. Actually take me to his hide out. He's really hooked up in Tijuana—very powerful man. No he's not a politician. He was the location manager for the movie *Traffic*. The movie. Yeah.

Now listen. I need to get down there right away. I just need some cash. Yeah, a $10,000-dollar-cash advancement. Hmm. Advancement. They're going to pay me. I'll pay you back. You don't trust me! It's me, okay it's a new, more responsible me. Listen, mother I'm not playing send me the money, so I fired you! *Mia culpa. Mia culpa, pardoname. Lo siento.* You got Chicano Alzheimer's, you forget everything but a grudge. Because I needed a different kind of assistant. Yes, a male one. Who told you that? They said I kissed him? They're lying. He kissed me. I was nearly violated. He's gay, I'm not. No, if your underwear is stretched out don't look at me. I'm not. I'm not gay. I swear I like girls. Just show me the money! Show me the money! Show me the money.

(Black out. Lights come up on BENNY as he reads a newspaper and sips coffee.)

BENNY: I been reading about the death penalty and you know, I been thinking about it. I have executed or killed or murdered or assassinated hundreds. Well okay. I'm bragging a little. I killed maybe only 60, 75 people. Sure, I ordered some deaths of at least a few families. But the point is I have killed, and I could be killed too. I could be executed. Sure I could be arrested and executed for my crimes, but not in Mexico.

There is no death penalty in Mexico. Thank God, we're civilized that way. But in the United States they have the death penalty and in Texas it's like fast food, they do executions like drive-through food orders. They give out death penalties like we give out beer on a Saturday night in Tijuana. But here in Mexico there are no executions. In Mexico we will not allow extradition to another country if that person could receive the death penalty. So America cannot legally kill me while I'm here. But I visit the United States a lot so I could get caught. You don't know. I don't always stay in Tijuana. I like to go the United States. I like to get sushi, buy ice cream, and walk in La Jolla, I even skin dive and feed the fish little peas. They love that. If I was caught in the United States, I could be executed.

So I'm watching CNN because I can't sleep and I hear about Raul Garza a convicted drug king pin that was executed in the United States. Now, listen to this, his last meal consisted of French fries, a steak and a Diet Coke. A Diet Coke. And now I really can't sleep because I'm thinking, *why in the hell would anyone have a Diet Coke with their last meal.* You are going to die. But this Raul Garza, he had a Diet Coke during his last meal and now I can't sleep. I wish he was alive. I'd kill him for keeping me up, but I can't because he's dead—because he had his last meal already. So I keep thinking about that and now I can't sleep because I see the crazy world I live in. I see the ironies all around me and I see how ridiculous it all is, but then it hits me.

Why do I have to die? I mean sure eventually we all die, but in my job most people die of bullet overdoses. They die in car accidents—the car swerves off the road after the bomb under the seat explodes. People want to kill me. Yeah, me. And not just respectable criminals but the FBI, George Bush, Jr. and Sr., the DEA, the Colombians, everyone wants to kill me. I love La Jolla. I love living in the United States. I have houses in La Jolla. I have ten—and believe me the prettiest home in La Jolla, it's mine, and if it's not, I'll buy it. Why should I die? Why can't I enjoy my money? Why can't I retire? Why not? I have built something on this border. I control this entire border. I control it better than the Border Patrol. I bring in all the drugs and now all the illegals. I now control the *coyotes.* I control that too. It's a business. I bought it last year. It's like a temp service for the United States. I have plenty of inventory. I'm running out of space to store my cocaine. I may have to have a sale. I got storage problems. I'm surrounded by it. I control the border. Why can't I control my own destiny?

No criminal wins. You might say, "But why can't I?" I'm going to watch CNN . . . watch some MTV on my big screen and relax and figure it out, because I can figure out anything if I try. I took an Anthony Robins seminar. I walked on coals. Anthony Robins is the great motivational guru. He can really motivate you, but then again so can I. I'll motivate the shit out of someone because I can. I'm Mr. Motivate.

(Lights down on BENNY. Lights up on BUFORD GOMEZ.)

BUFORD GOMEZ: I may be in a cell in Tijuana, but my mind is at one of my seminars. My body is here but my spirit is stuck in the air vent up there.

(Lights slowly change. BUFORD now is at his seminar.)

BUFORD GOMEZ: I want you all to keep studying the Border Patrol. Okay, where was I? We got these signs on our highways that look like this.

(A slide projected on the stages back wall/screen shows the border sign of a family running across a highway.)

BUFORD GOMEZ: It's the most embarrassing sign for any Mexican-American. We get to see this sign on the freeway going to work. It's embarrassing, and the sign is wrong. No Mexican man will ever run from his woman because when she catches him she'll cut his dick off. You'll be in your backyard with a flashlight saying, "Hey, help me look for something. I lost something. Hey don't touch that. Never mind it's a garden hose."

People die crossing the highway, people die crossing the desert, and people drown swimming in the ocean. But most people don't care about that. They just want us to stop them. They don't care how and if they get on over here. And guess what? The same God fearing tax paying people will hire them. No one wants to see us or the people I work with but they demand we do our jobs. We got some characters. They're all not normal like me. We had one guy . . . I used to tease him by saying, "Charlie is in the wire, Charlie is in the wire." Or I'd yell, "Incoming!" He had no sense of humor. If you can't laugh about your army days in Vietnam what are you going to laugh at? He had this twitch. He was a gun collector and civil war enactor who would want to enact the civil war? I know who's going to win! Mostly I'd stick with my partner; sometimes you need a break in the job. I wonder where they got me hidden.

(We hear the Mexican national anthem.)

BUFORD GOMEZ: Damn, I must be under the police station. There's an irony here I just can't see it. I had an incident that people still talk about out in the field—and I'm not talking about the chili con carne accident in the van during that stake out. I always have had a sensitive stomach. No, a different incident. I don't like to talk about it, but after that incident I was put on suspension for a week. We won't talk about that. So I traveled a bit. I know what you're thinking, *why leave the United States when you got Disney World?* So I went to Cuba once—I know it's illegal but I did. I was curious about Cuba. After arresting so many Cuban rafters you start to get curious. I like Cubans. I don't like Castro. He wins with this embargo. He won't stop people trying to leave his country. He encourages it. People in Miami they encourage it too. Only we discourage it. Cuba is only 90 miles from Miami. Some people say Cuba is paradise. The old Cubans living in Miami say, "I'm living in Miami just 90 miles from paradise."

Cubans are a fun Caribbean people, hard workers but they love to exaggerate. They say things like, "Back in Cuba I was head of the petroleum industry but in Miami I own a can of gas." I saw a Cuban exaggerating about how unlucky he was. He told one of his friends, "I'm so unlucky, Castro killed all my family." The other Cuban said, "That's nothing. I'm so unlucky Castro killed all my family with a single bullet and it was a ricochet. Now that's unlucky."

I have never told anyone this it's my greatest secret next to the time I faked an orgasm with my wife—it's a long story involving tapioca pudding. I was tired. The point is I went to Cuba. I was escorting a prisoner to Cancun—must've been a frequent deportation miles program winner. Well I had a week off—this was before I was married—I had a week off. It really wasn't a suspension more of a forced vacation. Well, I'm not talking about the incident. Before I was married I was a wild, two-stepping partying, beer drinking guy. I was wild then. I used to party real hard. Sometimes drink four beers, sleep in and not wake up and make my bed in a military fashion. I don't know how my saintly mother put up with me. Well, I was in Cancun and they had a deal to go to Cuba. So I'm thinking, *sure I always wanted to look at the Bay of Pigs just in case we go back again.* And I went to Cuba, Havana. I walked along the beach in my cowboy boots and underwear. I'm Mexican. We believe that no one can tell that you're wearing underwear; it looks like white trunks. I was wearing my Fruit of the Loom beach swimwear. I didn't have time to pack trunks.

So I went to Cuba and I met a girl. I called her Cuba Libre—Free Cuba. She was named after the drink, and she was beautiful. She must've worked in the tourism industry because she knew a lot of foreign men and she had plenty of dollars. Well she took me in her arms and sheltered me like a Cuban port to a ship in a hurricane. She gave me sanctuary and I loved her. *Cuba libre* means free Cuba. Some of them call it Cuba *mentirosa* because there is no true freedom in Cuba. These people risk 90 miles of the worst dangerous water on the earth to come here? You figure out why they do it, I been trying to figure it out for years. I think it's this, life wants to spread and get out and nothing will hold that back. When a baby wants to be born it will be born, life will find a way. When a bird wants to leave the nest it only knows to leave and it doesn't care where the nest ends and the sky begins. It flies.

I have never seen her again, but I think of Cuba Libre whenever I have the drink. I wish I had a drink right now. She set me free. She helped me forget all the bad things I see. Sometimes I get to see a thing that make me question what I'm doing here and that's bad because questioning is the enemy to military efficiency. Questioning makes you weak. You have got to be resolved in the Border Patrol. You must be a human wall, a barrier like the border you patrol, because it's either a barrier or a bridge. And ours is a barrier, it's something that keeps us separate. I will remember my oath to guard and protect the border; to hold up the wall. I'm doing fine, you hear me? I'm holding up this wall. Not even a cockroach will get in my cell. I'm still defending my border, my space from everything. You can't break Buford Gomez.

(Lights change. INEZ walks in drinking coffee.)

INEZ: I had an Anglo boyfriend and he invited me to go out with him. Well, on our first date he brought me to a Mexican restaurant. I thought to myself only an Anglo guy could think that up. I grew up on Mexican food. If I go out to eat give me sushi. My first date with my husband, we went line dancing and drank beers and it was fun. I'm with a redneck Mexican-American guy from Texas and it felt good. We had beers, line dancing and barbecue and some chips and salsa. It was simple things like that that made me love him. He knows who he is.

He's his job and I wish he was here. They tell me he's been captured by a gang of Narco traffickers. I thought his mother was drinking again but this time, it's for real. Since when does the police get caught by the crooks? This world is a bad place, why would I want to bring a child into it? But I do. I don't care that the ozone is depleting, the polar bears are starving, the ice caps are melting and we are over fishing and over mining. Overtaking everything. We are clear cutting and destroying the Amazon. The cities of Juarez and El Paso will run out of water in 20 years. We're drying up. I'm thirsty. I'm feeling really thirsty, so thirsty. Do you feel it?

The whole border is a war zone. The illegals that work in the United States at jobs no one else wants? These people are supporting villages in Mexico with the money they send home. Mexico is our biggest trading partner. They're our neighbors, not our enemy. They're our allies. What happens if we stop the illegals? Who's going to pick the crops and work for nothing? Not some yuppie kid. He's too busy starting an IPO, designing a web page, designing a new computer game, and then he's going to junior high. He's too busy to pick crops. And why not? Would anyone really want to work in the fields if you could work in an office making a thousand times more money? I know we Mexican Americans or at least Chicanos, we're all about the migrant field workers rights in the sixties, seventies, eighties, nineties . . . but I say let's not work in the fields anymore. Let them pick their own damn strawberries. That's the new Latino radical thought. We're not going to be those nice, happy colorful people. Pick your own damn grapes. We're in a computer workshop, we're learning real estate. Before you took our land and now we're selling it back to you.

Oh God, I'm talking crazy. I'm no radical. I'm no politician like Edward James Olmos. It's just with Buford gone, I'm losing it. They don't know where he is. They made demands. They will release Buford if Mexico releases all the Tijuana Cartels top drug lieutenants. Lieutenants. That sounds so military. When did we start a war on drugs? A war on illegal immigration? Do you know when my family crossed? My family crossed when there wasn't a border. We didn't cross the border, the border crossed us. The FBI said they'll find Buford but who believes in the FBI? I'd rather have the IRS looking for Buford not the FBI. Mother Gomez is in Tijuana looking for her boy. She says she knows some politicians. This family is falling apart. What if Buford does something foolish like try to escape? He's so brave. They found the tunnel Buford was investigating, seems like he went into the tunnel without calling for back-up. He's foolish and brave. They followed the tunnel and the other side had been dynamited closed. Buford hurt their operation, he's a hero. The FBI crime lab said it looked like Buford killed probably 20 guys before he was captured. Then again they said Buford was a black man. Seems like that's a normal mistake for the FBI. The FBI always seems to find a black man involved in all their crime scenes. What a coincidence. The FBI said they won't give in to the kidnapper's demands. This is the first crime of this sort ever. I said to the Border Patrol, "Can't you grab him like you did to Elian Gonzales?" If Buford was a little Cuban boy, they'd get him back in no time. I hope they're not torturing him. He has a low threshold for pain. He gets an ingrown toenail and he's practically crying. Damn, I hate waiting in the dark.

(Lights change. A steel sounding door creaks open. The MANIC HISPANIC enters with his hands up and a blindfold on.)

MANIC HISPANIC: This is great, a real exclusive. I'm going to meet Buford. They had me meet a strange man at this bar. He blindfolded me and tied me up and brought me here. It was so secretive and erotic. It reminded me of a date I once had . . . with a woman. . . . What? . . . I'm here to get the rights and I'm going to do it. Oh here? Just wait here? What is this, a loading dock? Is that flower? I love *postres* . . . That's . . . oh my God, is that all yours? Wow. Party like it's 1999. I have never. I'll wait here. I'll be fine. *(Beat)* I'm like a kid in a cocaine store. I mean candy store. You'll bring him here? Fine. Okay.

(He speaks into a cassette recorder.)

Scene opens up in a back room of a drug king pins lair. A man, Buford, is tied up in another room. Buford's back-up is surrounded by tons of cocaine. Camera pulls back to reveal this stark reality. We see someone snorting this cocaine casually, like this. *(He takes a big snort full and falls backward.)* This is pure. The quality is unbelievable. Oh my God this shit is great! I'm Tony the tiger. I feel grrrrreat. *(He laughs and snorts some more.)* Well, just a little more . . . it's research. It can't hurt. This is like an acting exercise, a "sense memory." I knew this unbelievable Puerto Rican methadone actor like Brando. He used "sense memory" all the time. Believe me they won't miss it. *(He takes an even bigger hit.)* They call me stormy Monday, but Tuesday's just the same. That shit is really good; the quality is quality, I mean that's real good. *(He talks very fast.)*

I'm feeling really confident that this is going to be a great movie. Now, I know how the guys felt during *Water World* and the movie *Pearl Harbor*. Yeah, you know now that I think about it? I'm confident this will be the greatest film ever made on the border. It's got conflict, sexy stars, lots of good shit. Wow, I feel really good. You ever wonder about black holes? Quantum physics? Shakespeare was such a genius and his stories are free. Hey, I know who we'll hire, Soderburg. Oh I know we'll get Paul Rodriguez and that "Crocodile Dundee" as partners on the border or Antonio Banderas to play Buford or Geoffrey Rush, Cher could be the mother. How about Melanie Griffith in a black wig as Buford's wife? Come on, Anglo women just don't age well. Wow, I see some lights. What's that music? You know I think I just heard my grandmother's voice and I can't understand her. She's speaking Spanish. Speak English! God, how many times do I have to tell you? *Abuela*, chill out. Should that bright white light be on? I'm feeling kind of "Sixth Sense-y" here, kind of "Ghost-y". I know what's happening to me. Oh no. This is not good. I'm out of my body. This is an out of body experience and oh my God! I'm looking down at my body. I'm floating over my body. Oh my God! Oh my God! I have a bald spot!

(The MANIC HISPANIC dies as the light slowly fades around him. Lights up on BUFORD GOMEZ)

BUFORD GOMEZ: Day ten of my confinement. There are other people with me; a journalist from Tijuana who had written an unflattering review about *Pearl Harbor*—Sony Pictures is more powerful than I thought; and some Chinese that could not pay the fare to cross. And a psychic, I don't know why he's here. It was a freelance kidnapping from someone else, it was cheaper to kidnap the psychic than call those 1-800 numbers. I'm learning about their operation and it's a big one. They even own a studio that has a connection with Sony Studios in Hollywood. I'm going to meet a producer who's going to negotiate my release. I'll start my hunger strike again but they got fish tacos and cold Corona beer on the menu. Those bastards are cruel; they keep sabotaging my hunger strike.

They told me a producer from a studio wants to do my story and a producer wants to meet me. I think it's that guy who came down pitching *Cops on the Border* TV show. I took him on a "ride-along" with me. I wonder who will play me. It should be Banderas or Tom Cruise, either one will do. I can't wait to see another person. I'm supposed to see him any minute now. Maybe he can stay a while. We could rent a movie. It will be good to talk English again.

(In the darkness we hear a woman—part of the pampered Mexican elite. Lights widen to reveal TELENOVELA THALIA, part of the Mexican upper-class.)

TELENOVELA THALIA: I'm shocked that life is more interesting than the *telenovelas*. What is happening to the world? I have a maid. She is the one with the braids that looks like an Indian. Maids, interestingly enough, don't look anything like Salma Hayek. Salma Hayek had a real maid. She probably had five growing up. Now she just acted like a maid on television. I played a maid on television for a 105 episodes. I was stunning. The evil rich man wanted me, the handsome rich male model wanted me, and the gorgeous surgeon wanted me. Even his sister with the slight moustache wanted me. But his parents would not allow it because I was a little Mexican Indian maid. I could have my maid here walking around serving margaritas in a bikini and no one would want her. *Telenovelas* are fantasy, they are distractions, and they give the people hope. Some say the plotlines are unbelievable, sure, but wasn't Cinderella? It's fantasy. Snow White was a fantasy. Princess Diana was a fantasy.

I'm supposed to be a happy wife; I have married well, but look where I am, in Tijuana at the border, at the *Frontera*. I should be in the capital.

I miss Mexico City. I miss the parties, the history of the city. There is history all around you. There is the place where Maria Candelaria sold flowers, the place where Enrique Iglesias first sang his big concert, or the place where his father Julio sang. There is the place where Juan Gabriel sang at the Belles Artes, the greatest concert hall in Mexico. I love Juan Gabriel. Oh, and there are pyramids if you like that sort of thing, but that's for the tourist. But come on, the history of Mexico is simple it's like a soccer game—Spaniards 51 points and Indians 0.

I'm here with my big screen TV. I get manicures almost hourly, we can afford it, and the workforce is very cheap here. I pay my help $10 dollars a day. That's it. Amazing, but not the lower-class workers. I played a poor Indian girl from my village—I still have my braids—a poor Indian girl who was loved by everyone, even the blind bullfighter with the big heart but bad sense of direction. He wanted me. It feels good to be wanted.

What is going to happen to us here? The border is getting more crowded. It's like we're all waiting to cross to the United States to get on with our lives. It's like purgatory. We're waiting. I want to be a crossover artist. I want to act in the United States. I want to do important work. I want to be on, on . . . soap operas there.

(We hear drilling; then it stops.)

Did you hear that? I hear things drilling underneath the house. I know what's going on, it's tunnels to the other side so they can bring drugs or people. I wanted to tell on them, to report it, but that would be rude. In Mexico there is an old saying, "In Mexico nothing ever happens but if something does happen, and then remember nothing happened." I'm not going to call the police. I don't want trouble. I'm married, I have had a good career and I married very well. Very well. He owns a *maquiladora* plant. He manufactures light bulbs. Light bulbs. I guess they're important. He's gone mostly so I'm here with Maria and three other maids and two gardeners and a driver. Our garden is only 50 feet long. Why do I need a gardener or this many maids? You know why? Because . . . it's because I can . . . I hope that doesn't sound shallow.

Would you like to see a scene from my *telenovela?* In this scene I'm a poor Indian maid Maria. I have come to fall in love with Enrique, the surgeon and male model and son of the governor of Michoacán.

(*As Maria:*) Enrique I love you!

(*Back to herself:*) God that was fun. Oh, those were the days. I loved those scenes. I could say, "I love you" with over a 100 different inflections and emotions. It's an exercise they teach you in the acting academy in Televisa. I love acting; it's so much more fun than life! Does that sound shallow?

(*MOTHER GOMEZ walks on stage. She is talking on the phone to an old style vaquero or cowboy, CONCEPTION GOMEZ who is offstage. He is heard overhead.*)

MOTHER GOMEZ: I need your help Conception. I need you to save my son.

CONCEPTION: I have a son?

MOTHER GOMEZ: I never wanted to tell you. I wanted to raise him in the United States.

CONCEPTION: Does he look like me? You sure he's my boy? No offense but when I met you, well pues you were working in Juarez as a . . . as a . . . a *puta*.

MOTHER GOMEZ: I was a hostess. You were the only man I was ever with. I swear to God! I was a virgin before I met you. I made money having guys buy me drinks. *Mi amor*, he's been captured by the Tijuana Cartel.

CONCEPTION: Ay, that's not good. Does he owe them money?

MOTHER GOMEZ: No, he's a good boy. He's named Buford Gomez he has your last name.

CONCEPTION: That's good. What does he do?

MOTHER GOMEZ: He's a Border Patrol Officer he's *La Migra*. Hello? Hello?

(*Sound of a phone off the hook. Lights down on MOTHER GOMEZ. Lights up on BENNY. He is beating on someone's chest.*)

BENNY: Oh my God, Mr. Negotiator? Mr.? Come on, breathe! Shit! What have you done? Did you use this cocaine? It's pure. You're not supposed to use this! Shit! You're supposed to wait here. This is a storage room. If I had you wait in the kitchen would you make an omelette? Wait, you stole from me you piece of shit! I'll kill you. No, I don't mean that, breathe. Come on, breathe. Oh damn.

(He puts the body down and walks down stage to speak to DIEGO who is offstage.)

Hey Diego, remove him. Damn, I got a bad feeling about this. Yeah, hey Jose, kill Diego. Yes, kill him. I know it's not his fault. I just want someone dead. Well he shouldn't have left him alone. Don't we have rooms without product? Well he should've stayed with him. Then he should've thought about it. Just kill him . . .

(We hear a door slam and footsteps.)

I don't like it when people die, and I had nothing to do with it. It makes me feel out of control. What are the odds of this happening? My negotiator is dead because of an overdose. No one has an overdose here. We sell drugs, we don't take 'em. What are the odds? I feel really unlucky. I'm going to call my psychic friend. I like calling my psychic friends even though they don't work. Really, they don't. It's bullshit. They're not psychic they're greedy. My psychic friend said I needed to get out more and put some excitement in my life. *(Beat)* Yeah they're good. The FBI called me psychotic, not psychic, because I killed without remorse. But I say I'm psychic because I can predict who is going to die.

Now I have a real problem. This guy is a real pain in the ass. People are going to think I killed him. You see how innocent people get blamed for things? Now you know why the death penalty is wrong. I got big problems. My hostage, who I never wanted in the first place, this Buford Gomez, is on a hunger strike. Yeah, he went on a hunger strike and somehow he leaked it to the press. But he's not on a hunger strike, he's gained weight. We took a picture of him and he sunk in his cheeks and sucked in his gut like those before-and-after pictures in gyms. He must have a publicist or something; the other side is making him look like a hero. "Return Buford!" They never wanted him before. See what being a hostage does. Elian Gonzales knows. When he was in America they wanted him back. They built a $2-million-dollar statue for him in Havana. Now, since he's back I bet no one gives a shit about Elian. I bet Elian's father is back there in Cuba saying, "Hello Castro, it's me, Elian

Gonzales' father. Elian, the kid that almost drowned off of Miami. Elian, E.. L . . . I.. I . . . Hello? Hello?" Castro should have put that $2 million from the statue into Elian's family before they left for the United States. Maybe they would have stayed.

Now everyone wants my hostage; they got Tony Orlando singing "Tie a Yellow Ribbon 'Round the Old Oak Tree." I have really had my confidence shaken. I mean psychic friends are not psychic. The media is full of lies and the heroes are not heroes. Buford Gomez, he did not fight valiantly. We shot at him once then he dropped his gun. I swear he was crying. He's not even a real American Border Patrol Agent. He's a *pocho*, he's Mexican-American. I'm Mexican I have an identity. There is no hyphen in my name. I'm not African-American, not Japanese-American, I'm not Mexican-American. I'm just Mexican, simple. My occupation, import/export dealer. I manufacture light bulbs. I'm a Mexican businessman, not a minority Mexican-American, Hispanic, Latino, Chicano businessman. See all those names are baggage. I'm free of baggage, I have a simple life because I have an identity. He's a hyphen! I'm going to kill him! Then he'll be a dead Mexican-American, Latino, Chicano, Hispanic border patrolman and I'll be a happy Mexican. Simple. Wake that Buford up. Wake him up! Yeah, open his door.

(*A pin spotlight shines in a corner where a chair sits. BENNY paces around the chair.*)

BUFORD GOMEZ: Who's there?

BENNY: How are you doing Officer Gomez? I'm sorry all this has happened to you, but you have cost me a great deal; I've lost my tunnel. It was a very big tunnel. I was proud of my tunnel. I now have product piling up all over the place. There is another border crack down. I got people piling up. I have you here. Now, what am I going to do with you?

BUFORD GOMEZ: I could go now, my Spanish is much better.

BENNY: Your government has a new non-negotiation policy.

BUFORD GOMEZ: I knew a Mexican-American is a bad bargaining chip. You guys should've got a white guy.

BENNY: I had someone that was going to meet you, but he's had an accident. We need a substitute. I know a priest. I called him. I'm going to tell him my demands. I need you to tell him you're well and that you want to go home.

BUFORD GOMEZ: What about the Hollywood producer?

BENNY: He had an accident. He's dead.

BUFORD GOMEZ: You killed him.

BENNY: See how people think. I did not kill him. You will read this statement telling people that you are well.

(BENNY hands him a paper to read. BUFORD throws it on the ground.)

BUFORD GOMEZ: I won't do it. You can't break me. All I have to do is give you name, rank, Social Security number.

BENNY: I don't want to break you. I want to get rid of you. You are like a hostage that no one wants. I would pay them to take you back.

BUFORD GOMEZ: Don't bother. They're going to break me out. We ain't going to let some criminal scum tell us what to do.

BENNY: You're not better than me. I did a little research on you. I asked around. Your mother worked as a whore in Juarez and you were born in Mexico and snuck over the border with your mother, the whore. You are a wetback, Buford, and your mother was a whore.

BUFORD GOMEZ: Don't ever call me a wetback. Take me out of these handcuffs and I'll fight you *mano y mano.*

BENNY: Wow, your Spanish is getting good!

BUFORD GOMEZ: Fight me one on one.

BENNY: If you want to fight, I'll let you fight a few of my men.

BUFORD GOMEZ: Just you. Me and you right now.

BENNY: I'm like that hockey player, Wayne Gretsky. I don't fight, I have other men fight for me. I'm going to leave now. It was a pleasure having you be my guest, but our time is over. Either they negotiate with me or I kill you.

BUFORD GOMEZ: Go ahead, kill me I'll show you how a Gomez dies—
with his boots on.

BENNY: No, you'll die naked with a plastic bag over your face.

(Lights change. TELENOVELA THALIA stands center stage in aerobics wear.)

TELENOVELA THALIA: I'm working out because it relieves stress.
Stress is the leading cause of death, except maybe not in Texas. In Texas
handguns are the leading cause of death. I would never want to live in the
United States; there is so much crime there. They have random acts of
violence. In Mexico there is no random violence. Our violence is planned.
We have a saying in Mexico and it goes like this, "In Mexico nothing
happens, but if something happens, remember nothing happened." *(Beat)*

My husband is under a lot of pressure lately. He seems stressed. He can't
concentrate. We don't make love anymore. I'm in shape, I look good, no?
Look at me, every man and some very aggressive women want to have
me. I have worked my whole life to be a mother, a wife, a *telenovela* star,
and a humanitarian; that's not easy. I have worked hard to create glamour.
Look at the class, the style in my home. Look around my house. Look at
those reclining jaguars against the wall—he chose those. He has no class.
You see them against the wall that's a jungle motif. I read *Martha Stewart*
magazine like it's a religion. I make dinner that he doesn't eat. I made a
napkin doily thing that he could care less about.

He's always gone working in the United States. He has to be careful, he
has an outstanding warrant; he told me an ex-wife in the United States
was trying to sue him so when he goes to the United States it's very secret
and I never go with him. He has security around him 24 hours a day
because he's an important businessman. There is crime here, kidnapping!
Well sure, I know the rumors, but that's not true, he's not that man, he
manufactures light bulbs. He makes car parts for Volkswagens, and he
exports chili peppers to the United States. He is not a drug dealer! Every
time someone sees a rich Mexican they think drug lord. Well he's not one.
Sure, he knows some from a distance, but they have totally exaggerated
him. I know about the reward for him but that's not him, that's another
man with his same name. It's a common mistake. The picture looks like
him sure but come on, Latino man, dark hair, and brown eyes. Oh maybe
a 100 million fit that profile.

It's like me. They once said things about me when I was on the soap opera. The magazines said how I was loose, how I was a slut, how I was evil, but I knew that was my character. That was not me. That was the character I played. We all play characters. Some people so identify with their characters that they become them. I knew I was not a bitch—that was my role. My character now, I'm a wife, this is my role, this is my character. My husband is not a drug lord, that is not his role not his character. I'm not a bitch, he's not a drug lord. Maria! Bring me my damn margarita! I'm not a bitch. I used to play one on TV, that's all, in the *telenovelas*. I'm a housewife.

(Lights change. A very dead MANIC HISPANIC stands with a white light glowing about him. Heavenly music plays. He seems angelic and at peace.)

MANIC HISPANIC: So, I'm floating around here for a while. No one pays attention to me. I felt like how I did when I first joined Sony studios in the Latino division—that was tough. I didn't speak a word of Spanish. I had to meet other Latino executives and we would be at these gala events and I would just laugh at the stories they would tell. They would always start with the question, "Do you speak Spanish?" And I'd say, "*Sí*." Yes. Then they would tell me a joke and when they would finish I would just start to laugh. I would laugh really hard. Well, after a while it gets back to my boss that everyone likes me. I was doing great. Then one time I'm at this party and this guy asks, "Do you speak Spanish?" And I say, "Yes." And he starts to tell me a joke about El Salvador and he's good. We're an expressive people. We are an emotional people. He's acting it out and everything, he has tears in his eyes, and then he stops, so I start to laugh really loud. It ends up he was telling me about El Salvador where they had just had a devastating earthquake and his whole family had been killed. Well, I get fired from Sony Latino and I'm about to be hired by another studio and they say they heard a vicious rumor that I don't speak Spanish and they tell me the "El Salvador earthquake story," but I think fast and say I speak Spanish. I just hate El Salvadorians. This executive looks at me then smiles and says, "I'm Guatemalan, I hate those *pupusa-*eating bastards too." And he gives me the job.

Oh, it feels so freeing to be dead. First off no taxes, I don't have to keep receipts. They can't fire you. They can't hurt you. What can they do, make you alive again? Also, I get to watch the world live. People are like cable channels, it's so fun. I get to see the real *Sex in the City*, the real *Sopranos*.

I get the *Real World* MTV-style 24/7. I get to see the real *Survivors*. They are right here on the border. TV is boring. I can see the real deal, 24 hours a day. I don't need to sleep or eat. I don't need anything. I'm at the border so I got a front-row seat between heaven and hell, between Mexico and the United States, between earth and sky. I'm in purgatory. I'm in between everything. I could move on but I'm content, I'm having fun, afterlife has really taught me how to enjoy life. I can play around. My favorite thing to do is to contact psychics and lie to them. I get them really convinced they're hearing my voice and I just lie to them. They think they got some spiritual insight and they don't. It's not God talking to them it's me! I think I started two cults already! They worship Madonna and Martha Stewart as prophets of a God named me. I told one psychic to borrow from the mob and bet on a horse that I overheard the trainers say had leukemia. The horse lost and the psychic lost all the mob's money and was killed, isn't that tragic. I can't believe the horse died. It was so sad. I love animals. Sometimes I go to parks and stand next to families and believe I'm one of them, but they can't see me, but I can see them.

You get to see a lot of things when you're dead. You see tragedies, you can hear how people think and you know something? If you think I'm shallow, you should hear half the things I hear in people's thoughts. I went to a modeling agency and it was totally silent. Silent. I think that most people are waiting for life to happen. I was on my latest deal, I was always developing something that never went anywhere; they call that development hell. I was waiting for life and then death happened out of nowhere. I thought, "Drug overdose," how cliché, but there are worse ways to go. One guy I met died in the arms of a Tijuana prostitute and he was a gay civil rights activist so his homosexual partner had to find out that was he straight, what a shock. He was straight. He acted gay for the political benefits. His gay partner was so embarrassed. He was cheating on him with a woman, yeah, strange, hmm. Another guy I saw died while stealing electricity. He had come up with the bright idea to tap into the electrical line from a nearby electrical pole with his hand. He thought a rubber glove was all he needed. A woman I saw died during an herbal wrap and had a heart attack while wrapped too tight. But she looked fabulous! Another guy died in the desert. He was crossing over to the United States. He had survived by drinking his own urine to survive. He even stole someone else's urine to live. He made it. But a year later he was killed by a drunk driver. Now this is the strange part, the drunk driver was driving drinking his own urine mixed with vodka when he hit him.

So, I'm here, I no longer have any worries, I can go wherever I want to, but everywhere I go it's the same—there is the living and the dead. Sometimes I can't tell the difference between the living and the dead, especially here. But then again who can? It's Tijuana, the border between the living and the dead, the legal and the illegal, the Mexican and the American.

(Lights change and Buford Gomez's father CONCEPTION GOMEZ walks on stage in a cowboy hat. A vision of the Old Mexico.)

CONCEPTION GOMEZ: I been thinking maybe I should not have hung up on her. She may have been a *puta*, but she's the mother of my child. I loved her. I had a boy with her. I have a boy after all these years. His name is Buford . . . *Ay, ¿porqué?* Buford? What kind of boy of mine could be called Buford?

I was wild when I was young. I was a macho back in my day. I looked good with my cowboy hat and boots and I was wild. I loved being a cowboy back in Sinaloa. I loved our life, our *corridos*, our songs. I have heard *corridos* sung about our life. *Corridos* are folk songs; in English they're called country music. In our *corridos* the same thing happens to us as to the rednecks. We lose our ranch, our dog dies, and our wife dies too. Now they are making *corridos* about the border and about coyotes running people and drugs. It's all changing.

I loved being a rancher singing *corridos*; I had always hoped they would make a *corrido* about me, but it's too late, I'm old. I was a good *vaquero*, but the rancho I worked on was never good to me, it never made much money, and I was never making money. But who cares when you looked good. I looked like Pedro Infante. I was good looking when I was thinner. I used to run cattle and I made good enough money. A lot of my family was ranchers. Then they started losing land to *marijuaneros*. They grew marijuana and they had guns and took over. I lost my ranch to a *político* that wanted it. At that time, Mexico was very corrupt, but it's always been that way. *Pues*, it started with Cortez, Mexico never got over that, all our problems are because of Cortez. He put the question in all of us. What are we? Indian? European? And we come to hate one side of ourselves. And when we go to the United States, what are we? Mexican? When are you truly American? Pues, I wonder. But, I don't wonder too much because I know who I am. I'm Conception Gomez. I have never once questioned that.

I'm Conception Gomez. I was born in Sinaloa under a clear blue sky. I smelled a fire nearby with tortillas cooking and my first taste in my mouth was the tequila my father put on my lips to bless me. I'm Conception Gomez. There has never been a border and there has never been a fence in my life. I'm a cowboy, a *vaquero*, and we hate fences. We like wide, open spaces. We judge a man by who he is how and how he acts; not how much he owns but how much he gives away. We judge a man by his word. Well, I keep mine. My boy is Buford Gomez. I may not like what he does, but my blood, it flows in his veins. He has my blood and his mother has my word. He needs me so I know what to do. Zapata said, "Better to die on your feet than live on your knees." You see my knees? I never have been on them. You see my boots? I have worn them out by always standing on them, but, it's the Tijuana Drug Cartel. You might say, "How can one man stand against them?" I don't know, you'll have to wait to hear my *corrido*. This will make one hell of a song.

(A shaft of light illuminates BUFORD.)

BUFORD GOMEZ: I have been catching all these cockroaches. I got about a 100. I've named them. Am I losing it or just keeping my hunting instinct in shape? *(Beat)*

So they're going to kill me. Well, there could be worse things that could happen to me. Like being fired from the Border Patrol. I love being an agent. To be a Border Patrol Agent you got to develop cat-like reflexes. I'm like a cat. Not just because I sleep a lot, I do. I'm just like a cat because of my hunter instinct. When you have a cat bring you home a mouse, that is the cat's way of saying, "I love you. Here's a mouse eat it. Come on, eat it. Well, you ungrateful human." Well, when I bring in a subject it's my way of saying how much I love you, America. I'm just like a cat; I'm more active at night, I'm nocturnal, and I'm a good hunter. Some people claim we have racial profiling here at the Border Patrol, that's not true. Here are some slides of suspects.

(A slide of a Mexican guy, with dark hair and short moustache that reads "Suspect Ramirez" is projected onto a large screen onstage.)

BUFORD GOMEZ: This man was a stopped for a broken taillight. Just a coincidence.

(The next slide: the same man with his hands in the air.)

BUFORD GOMEZ: Next time he was stopped for tinted windows. Just another coincidence. Another time he was stopped because he was seen in the neighborhood just too many times without a single garden tool with him—ends up Professor Mindiola has a very strong temper. We do not racial profile. It just so happens more dark people are pulled over statistically because of all their traffic infractions. My people love to add accessories to their cars. It's all strange coincidences. One time I found an illegal at the side of the road. He had cowboy boots, a cowboy hat on and he was dead. He got run over crossing the 5 freeway. He looked a lot like me. We are warned about that phenomenon where you begin to relate to your enemy. I began to relate to illegal Mexicans. They wanted the same things; we all want a home, a job, a family, some dignity, respect, love. We all want that and this man wanted it too. We put up signs to warn people, *"Por amor de dios, no cruzen la autopista."* But they cross the highway and sometimes get run over. He looked a lot like me.

I have always wanted to be a cowboy, I don't know where I get that. I love everything about cowboys. I even started smoking Marlboros to be like a cowboy. Cowboys smoke Marlboros. I swear I smelled the wide, open spaces when I smoked 'em. Well it smelled like the wide open spaces after a brush fire, but I felt I was in Marlborough country. Being a cowboy is about freedom; all you need is what you got with you—a horse, transportation, cattle and food. Move cattle, purpose. Cowboys got purposes, of course there are no Indians to fight no more, but who really wants to fight Indians? I've been to war after war, you never want to fight again. Besides, I'd be a modern cowboy. I'd have an assault rifle. Sitting Bull would have been called Running Bull if I had my AK. If you have an AK, it's always a good day. I'm getting philosophical here; like guys at Star Trek conventions. Would Spock win in a fight or Captain Kirk? If you have the answer, you're a nerd but I want to be a cowboy, and that illegal wanted to be a cowboy too. He wanted to be free, to work the range. He wanted to be independent, get respect, to have a purpose, that's why he crossed. I just stared at him for the longest time, him looking up at the stars, eyes wide open, dead. He was looking right at me. Like saying, "Buford Gomez, I'm a cowboy and so are you. Why you helping them hurt me? 'Cowboys, hate fences. We like wide, open spaces.'" I felt bad, real bad, but I put it away deep. I put that feeling deep under my flak vest and I forgot about it.

So then, I'm riding along that night near Oceanside, near Del Mar, and something strange happens . . . we find a cougar in the road, dead. Someone had run that cougar over. Now, what is strange is that cougars are normally not that far inland. They stay up near that Marine base, Camp Pendleton. He must have wandered down looking for a meal. Maybe he found an old cougar trail and instinctively followed it? Cats— and even big cats—all work from instinct. He was killed for just trying to live just like that Mexican. So my partner starts crying and I started crying looking at that big cougar dead in the road. Then I realize we didn't cry for the man, we cried for the cougar. Then I got mad. Mad at myself. And then I returned to the check point and realized I'm not busting people that look like me, I'm not going to be the barrier, the fence for my people. My supervisor Chung Lee said, "Buford, why you got to think, don't think allest people." He has a problem with "R" sounds. Well I lost it. I said, "I'm not getting people that look like me. I'm getting all the aliens that don't." They may be illegal Canadians stealing hockey jobs from American boys. That blonde family from Minnesota could be illegal Norwegians. That blue-eyed, blonde, tall man in the Mercedes Benz could be an illegal German stealing a rocket scientist's job from a good old American boy. Hey you, Gunter. Get out of the car. Yeah, I'm talking to you Gunter. You got a green card? A *carte de verde*? No? Just what I thought . . . I got's myself an illegal. You see folks if the original Mexican Border Patrol had stopped more aliens, California, New Mexico, Texas, Colorado and parts of Utah would still be Mexico.

Well, I got suspended and that's the "incident." They were dragging me away. I was yelling, "Let go of me! I'm not finished! I want to give him a cavity search, he might be hiding a little Irish man! Let me go, I'm not finished!" *(Beat. Buford calms down.)* That was the "incident." It wasn't a big deal. Seems like they have those incidences from Mexican-American Border Patrol men, black Compton police men, Italian FBI officers in New Jersey looking into organized crime, and Chinese traffic officers 'cause they're giving driving tickets to their people a lot. Asians can't drive. They can't drive! That may be a generalization, but generalizations work. They have these incidences with Cuban Border Patrol men in Miami, and white police men arresting white guys in Georgia. People start to identify with the enemy. It's called human sympathy syndrome. Now we try to keep sympathy to a minimum here, but it's just not working. *(Beat)* One of my cockroaches died—Fredrico. He was the one with a sense of humor. Am I losing it? No. I was right, Fredrico was the funny one.

(Lights change. New characters—the radical MECHA MADNESS guys—stand on stage. They're two young homeboys, one clearly younger than the other. The older homeboy has flunked junior college repeatedly. They wear Che tee shirts and brown berets. The MECHA MADNESS characters may be played by the actors playing BUFORD and BENNY.)

MECHA MADNESS #1: Okay, listen up. This meeting will be conducted in English, the hated language of our oppressor, because my Spanish is real bad—but I got a "C" in Spanish because that stands for Chicano. I'm pure Chicano. I was created by the rape of our indigenous mothers by our oppressive Spanish fathers. Death to Julio Iglesias and . . . .

MECHA MADNESS #2: Enrique.

TOGETHER: Fuck you.

MECHA MADNESS #1: Okay, we have had some more scandals besides the famous dance scandal where we had low attendance and no one came except us two. But it still was a good dance, we danced slow. Remember? We had oldies playing, "Now and Forever." We had some bad attendance—only us two, but we still had fun. I got a hickey.

MECHA MADNESS #2: I got laid.

(They look at each other.)

TOGETHER: But we did it for *La Raza*.

MECHA MADNESS #1: Recently we have spent our funds on a campaign to drive out the white man. We have an army of 20,000 strong. Twenty thousand strong and big.

MECHA MADNESS #2: I'm big boned. That's all. Big boned. It's muscle.

MECHA MADNESS #1: It's the fat on top of them muscles that I'm talking about. Leave the carnitas alone! I know you been cheating during our hunger strikes. We all need to be ready to take back Aztlán. We need to be ready. The border is heating up, the white man is trying to invade Mexico under the pretense to get back one of their agents of oppression. A Border Patrol Agent, a field agent working in the field—whereas the house agents live in the plantation house along with the Cuban Republicans. We will not let this happen! Bush has oppressed our people for too long. He bombed Puerto Rico—sure it was a Navy firing range, but that's just practice for his invasion of East Los Angeles.

MECHA MADNESS #2: Word, word, preach it. Jeb is just like that *vato* on the *Beverly Hillbillies*.

MECHA MADNESS #1: Jeb. He even married one of our own. She is a Malinche. He is oppressing her, making half-breed Latinos, diluting our pure Raza. We will not let that happen. Let our people go or let us go to Mazatlán. Free up our funds. We are planning an "America Out of Puerto Rico" rally but we are no longer in solidarity with our Puerto Rican brothers because one of them stole my girl again. That fast-dancing-*mofongo*-eating bastard took my girl, so it's on. I want a show down. I will use my Aztec style of fighting called ASTACKY ATTACKY. It involves some real old moves. I will demonstrate.

(He does some strange moves. Then he gets a cramp.)

MECHA MADNESS #2: Walk it out, homes.

MECHA MADNESS #1: That was a flying killer eagle move. We are pure Chicano with our army of 20,000 members—we would've been 30,000 but most didn't want to pay the $30 dollar MEChA dues. Twenty thousand. But that was over 30 years ago. Some of them are lying low. We call them "brown gophers," ready to dig their way to the top and attack the white man. The white man is scared of your leader and the FBI is watching me. I confronted the FBI agent watching me, but he claimed he was mall security and he acted like he did not know about my file. They got a file on me. It's so secret even they don't know it exists, but it's all good. If you got any questions give me a call. Right now I'm still living with my mother, so never call me past ten.

MECHA MADNESS #2: She will kick his ass.

MECHA MADNESS #1: Okay, now we are having more scandals . . . but people we got the white man on the ropes! Soon Aztlán will be ours! We funded a flyer campaign with all of our chapters' money. It was either that or try to get a "Que Loco" comedy tour to come here, or rent *Selena* again. Well, we funded some propaganda—we used all our chapters' cash and some of my father's money. I liberated some of his funds for us. After a couple of Tecate beers he don't know what checks he's writing. This is our flyer. We made over two million of 'em.

(A slide is projected on the stage's wall of a flyer that reads "Whites gets out! This is ARE land—la Raza!" It is placed over a map of California.)

MECHA MADNESS #2: Oh, excuse me homes, but ummm . . . But you spelled that wrong.

MECHA MADNESS #1: You sure? Damn.

MECHA MADNESS #2: Yeah, I been up in this junior college now five years. I took Spanish as a second language. Yeah, English is my first and only language.

MECHA MADNESS #1: Okay, we will be having another fundraiser to make more flyers. Who wants to be on the flyer committee? Okay, Haji, how's your English? Good, you design the flyer. Okay, we got to have another car wash. Anyone got a car?

(Sounds of people crowding into a room. A masculine woman walks to a podium on stage. She adjusts herself. She's a Janet Reno type, but less feminine.)

CAPTAIN JOHNSON: Okay, please settle down, get your coffee and donuts and sit down. This is our briefing on our situation at the border. Things have really heated up here. We will not negotiate for Officer Gomez, but we will find our officer. Raul, can you get me coffee?

INDIAN HAJI: Yes, my friend, I mean *amigo*, sir. Right away.

CAPTAIN JOHNSON: Oh, you want to say something? Oh, of course. Before I speak people, I think we have something important to do first. Mr. Barnes?

(GREG BARNES a very white serious looking man with a mission.)

GREG BARNES: Thank you for allowing me to speak. A big hand for Captain Johnson, she's doing a great job. Gentlemen, ladies, members of the Aryan race, I'm speaking to you. You are the foot soldiers against the loss of American sovereignty. We are being invaded by Mexico now. More than ever Latinos are telling us what to do. The bombing of Vieques was right. We used to be able to bomb all over Puerto Rico at will, but now we are stopping! Why? We are caving in to the wishes of Puerto Ricans and Chicano MEChA activists who are causing that *liberal* President Bush— the lad who's got Latino special interests. He wants Latino voters, but there are millions that are voting and they're not even citizens. We have trouble, folks. I'm talking about the loss of American sovereignty.

Recently a member of Mexico's president Fox's cabinet said he hoped the Mexicans here would help Mexico first. He wants them to invest back in Mexico. If you are here, America is first, second and third. He said, "Mexico is first." Not America first. We have had incredible economic growth in this country, but that's a lie. That's a lie because I'm still living at home. I lost my wife to a Latino salsa instructor from Rubio's. He was an illegal. His family snuck over in 1840. There are 20,000 MEChA soldiers in school right now. They're in Los Angeles—which I guess is Spanish for "it's ours." President Bush, that liberal, was quoted as saying we want "safe immigration." His brother was seduced and even married a Mexican woman. He's not thinking clearly. Don't you see? They're seducing us with their sexy women, music, dance, culture, and the food's pretty good. Thank God we still control television. We have agents of our brotherhood that have vowed never to let them on television. Thank God for our network—Aryan brotherhood. Oh sure, maybe you'll see them people on reruns of *I Love Lucy*, but that's the exception, because it's *I Love Lucy* not "I Love Desi."

Bush wants safe immigration. They're putting up emergency watering stations so people don't die of thirst. The desert is designed to kill people; we put up watering holes they'll survive! Isn't that defeating the purpose of a dangerous desert designed to kill? In the old days there was no safe immigration. God put up a natural border like the Rio Grand River and the desert to drown or kill anyone trying to get here that was not holding a first class ticket coming from spring break in Puerto Vallarta. Safe and orderly? You got Cuba, China and Mexico forming an axis to invade America. Let's just give them the keys to our homes. China is using agents in the Panama Canal. Mexico says that their citizens are expanding the borders of Mexico, and they are. There are Latinos in Virginia for God sakes! What is that? Expanding their borders? They got a radical group called MEChA Movie Estudiante de Aztlán; they think the Southwest is part of Aztlan, Mexico.

The border is like a sponge, people. God it's scary. They have Spanish TV here taking up my signal. There are Latinos everywhere. Walt Whitman said, and I quote, "America is not merely a nation but a teaming nation of nations." Walt Whitman was a fag. You want a fag deciding where your border is? Democrats and liberals are taking these Mexicans and using them against us. We lost Orange County, what's next? Sure the Republican election was won by a few Republican votes in Florida—thank God for the Cubans. They're Republican and voted our way, but Cubans, you voted, so thanks for the votes, now you can leave. I swear to God I need a passport and a Spanish dictionary just to visit Miami. The fruit fly . . . who brought them here? Illegals! They carry them here as pets. They got little cages for them! I've seen it. Hoof and mouth tacos they are packing in their lunch pails. Trucks with no breaks and a little Virgin de Guadalupe statue on their dashboard as their only form of insurance.

CAPTAIN JOHNSON: Um, thank you Reverend Barnes. But I thought you were just going to say a word of prayer for Officer Gomez.

GREG BARNES: Sure, he's in my prayers. I'm out of here. Raul, get me another margarita.

(He exits.)

CAPTAIN JOHNSON: Okay, here is our search radius. So far Mexico will not let us invade or assist in looking for Officer Gomez; it seems last time we came we took about 2,000 miles of their land back with us. Well, I guess some people can't seem to get over history. Come on Mexico! Will we have to use our informants and criminals to help us find where we think Officer Gomez is being held?

As for the PR war, we're winning! We have galvanized a lot of people and earned some sympathy for Officer Gomez, but there was that hostage negotiator that offered to talk to the cartel. He was a Latino executive who knew some people in Tijuana from the film *Traffic*. Seems the location manager from the film *Traffic* found our man before we did. Sure, that was an academy award–winning film but they really didn't talk about the Border Patrol or the FBI much. Those guys will never work with our department—you screw me once, shame on you; twice, shame on me. We are not going to let some Mexican police get the glory. We're going to get him back; he's one of our boys.

We have some leads that place Buford anywhere from at a bar in Tijuana to under the police department, to a basement of a *maquiladora* plant that manufactures light bulbs. We got a man to find and I'm not talking about my love life. He might not be holding up too well, some say he could be a victim of mind control. They say they could be torturing him. As for the producer . . . he was found murdered, seems like they filled his body with cocaine. That sick bastard killed a man of peace. I have a letter from him. A blah, blah, blah . . . we are all scared, all scared, I'm not Latino or anything else. . . . Well, it was touching. He is survived by his mother and, well, something like that really brings it home. This is a joint task force FBI, DEA, Border Patrol and Customs. Hold on, some late-breaking news. I see we're ready to go on in. Gentlemen, we're going to get him out. Let's roll . . . . lock and load. Gentleman, it's going down tonight.

(Lights down on CAPTAIN JOHNSON. Lights up on BUFORD GOMEZ looking more disheveled in his little cell.)

BUFORD GOMEZ: They tried to use mind control, filling me with lies saying my mother was a . . . That's ridiculous, and that I was born here. I'm an American citizen. They say they're going to kill me. I won't crack. I'm an officer of the United States. I love my job protecting the border. That's right I remember *(Beat)* Where was I . . . ? Yes, now I remember. The Border Patrol was established 75 years ago in El Paso when a group of officers formed the Border Patrol to defend our borders from the Chinese. Yes, the Chinese, not the Mexicans. The Chinese were coming to America to work on the railroads back then. Seems at that time most Mexicans were already here. We have a Border Patrol museum where you learn these facts and you can buy mugs, coffee cups, hats. Now they're trying to find enough money for the Border Patrol memorial for our fallen comrades. Over 13 Mexican-Americans have been killed in the border patrol. Thirteen. That's a lot. We have served.

I know there are some white American groups scared about a militant group trying to reconquer the Southwest. The *"reconquista"*—that's what they call it. Well come on, that's stupid, there is no *"reconquista"* there is only Rosarita. Rosarita refried beans and Cinco de Mayo and some block parties in East Los Angeles because—I'm going to tell you a secret—they're worried about Mexicans taking back the Southwest. Mexicans are not taking back the Southwest! They don't need to. They're already here. They have been here for a long time. The difference is no one paid attention to them 'til now. No one ever noticed them. You never saw Latinos; they weren't on TV. The Latinos did not vote so politicians didn't notice them. No one noticed them. People just thought that Mexicans named all the cities like Los Angeles and San Francisco; they built some missions and just left. They served you fast food, mowed your lawns, watched your children, and then just disappeared. California is like a rich guy coming home and seeing some Mexican mowing his lawn. He thinks, "Wow, I didn't know someone mowed my lawn, I thought it just grew short."

It's like this; people are just now noticing Mexicans. People think Mexicans are like those Keebler elves that bake their cookies. They're a mystical people that do all the work while you're sleeping. Then in the morning they're gone. Listen people, they're all around you. They're around all of us. I'm one of them. Sure I'm American but I'm one of them too. I'm reevaluating my life. I'm seeing things a little different. Think about it: 35 million Latinos, then add about five million illegal aliens, and then let's add Mexicans that don't show up in statistics, people that are half Latino . . . You just don't notice them, and neither did I. But after being in a dark room for 20 days you get to think or go crazy. And I been thinking, or maybe I'm thinking crazy. But I been thinking this border can't keep them out. Where do these people want to live? In a whites-only area called Gringolandia? I guess that's called Utah. Would that really make them happy? I don't think so! Listen folks, the Latinos are here, but stop worrying, they're not taking over, you are.

America makes Americans. That's what they do. No one totally keeps their culture. Hell, we took some uptight ass witch burning pilgrims landing on Plymouth Rock and 200 years later we turned them into trailer trash on Jerry Springer. Don't worry folks, we got Hollywood, the world propaganda machine deciding what we eat, drink, and drive. America is the world leader in making Americans. Sure they become American real fast, and they will continue to if we let them.

Some radical white guys think it's wrong that we stop bombing Vieques in Puerto Rico. Come on, I've been to Vieques. It's just a little island. We can find and bomb another island. How about Maui? Manhattan? Long Island? You bomb Maui and those Republicans would be lobbying in Washington. Some people on the border say Bush is too soft. Some say he is soft because he's listening to Latino voters. So what if he is? It's called democracy. Democracy, which by the way was invented by a bunch of Greek homos. Democracy. It's what every Latino has fought for including me, and anyone who is against democracy is just plain un-American.

So this is what I been thinking. I been thinking that no border wall has ever worked. Hadrian's Wall in England was built by the Romans and it did not work. It kept not one barbarian back from Rome. The Berlin Wall was torn down. It did not work. The Great Wall of China that was made to keep out the barbarians and the Mongols failed, they eventually had a Mongol emperor of China. Walls, fences, just don't work. *(Beat)* What am I saying? What the hell am I doing? I have not lost it. Ask the cockroaches in my cell. Francisco tell them that I'm fine. *(Beat)* Maybe I'm wrong or . . .

(SFX: Gunshots are heard.)

BUFORD GOMEZ: . . . Or maybe I'm losing it. Maybe it was just brainwashing that's making me think these obviously wrong ways of thinking. Because they are breaking me out! Forget what I just last said. I'm back to my old self.

(SFX: More gunshots are heard.)

BUFORD GOMEZ: God bless America. Well, that sounds like the sweet smell of freedom! I'm going home folks! I know what I'm going to do, I'm going to get my woman pregnant because life has got to get out, and Buford Gomez has got to get out of here. I'm making a run for the border. I'm going back to being a lean mean, deporting, machine. I'm Buford Gomez! I put the "ill" in the word illegal! I'm the best at the arrest. I'm the elite on the beat.

(SFX: more gunshots are heard. In the darkness BUFORD GOMEZ runs offstage. Lights up on CAPTAIN JOHNSON.)

CAPTAIN JOHNSON: It seems as though we did not actually raid where Buford Gomez was being held; we did raid very close to where he was being held, which is very good! I see the positive in this joint task force raid. It seems our Mexican counterpoints, along with us, raided the

Mexican NRA headquarters for Baja California. Carlos Gomez was quite armed, so we were able to make an arrest. Seems Carlos Gomez had some outstanding traffic tickets. Well, the point is the DMV was very thankful. That's interdepartmental cooperation, but at our interdepartmental softball tournament this week they may not get so lucky. GO green!

So, as for the latest, it seems an Officer Gomez was retrieved in San Ysidro dazed and confused. He was released during what witnesses describe as a gun battle between him and an old man in a cowboy outfit. I believe that a *vaquero* and members of the Tijuana Drug Cartel were engaged in this gun battle. The head of the cartel was killed along with numerous suspects. In a hail of gun fire Buford Gomez escaped, and, using tactics taught at the Border Patrol survival training school, got a cab and was dropped off at the border. He did get in a fight with the cab driver; it seems Officer Gomez did not have any tip money. Well, after heroically subduing the cab driver, Officer Gomez evasively blended in with some under-aged, drunk, high school kids and crossed the border into freedom. As for the *vaquero* who attacked the Tijuana Cartel . . . ? Well, he was killed, but it seems there is a *corrido* about him called, "The Cowboy from Sinaloa That Attacked the Tijuana Cartel." But this is just a rough translation.

(Music is heard. A corrido with a female singer.)

CAPTAIN JOHNSON: *(Singing/Translating)* I come from Sinaloa with a pistol in hand, I have come to kill a drug dealing man. I'm the cowboy from Sinaloa named Conception Gomez. I rode to the home of the Tijuana Cartel on a horse that was grand with my pistol blazing and my voice singing strong. I've come for the drug lord and kill all that I can. I'm the baddest motherfucker oh mother-of-pearl in these damn hills. My balls are big as watermelons . . . My . . . *(Beat)* I can't repeat this word. My *blank* is long . . . Geez . . .

(She stops singing.)

CAPTAIN JOHNSON: It's a *corrido*. They're all about the same. You get the picture. So, we're letting Officer Gomez get some much needed rest. He was injured during the fight with that Tijuana taxi driver that wanted the tip. That woman used some pretty unsavory fighting techniques. She had really long fingernails and used to live in the United States, by the alias of "La Sad Girl" from Pico Rivera, but Officer Gomez is fine.

Oh, by the way, we did apprehend an illegal at the hotel where we had a command post. He was named Raul Garza. He was a Mexican with a fake green card right under our nose. He was serving us coffee. Well, he was deported back to Tijuana. When will they learn? That is all, good night and God speed.

(Lights change. As they almost go black, in the darkness we hear BENNY. A corrido plays overhead.)

BENNY: They love to make songs about Narco traffickers. You believe a *corrido* or a government report? I'm not dead. I'm free. I'm free for once in my life. I'm truly free. It's like I'm born again. This has been a wonderful experience for me, better than walking on coals. I have really had a revelation. I saw something incredible. I saw an old man in a *vaquero* outfit on a horse with six guns shooting at me. It was like those old Vicente Fernandez movies. I thought I had seen it all but I haven't, it was humbling for me. I learned a lesson. I was prideful. I was wrapped up into myself. But he was like a vision. Pure and free and I was hiding. I'm the most powerful man in these Americas because I'm the gatekeeper. I control it all. And I'm just hiding in Tijuana, and I'm not free in the United States or here. So I made a call. I made a deal.

If the President of the United States could stop 50 percent of the flow of illegals and drugs to the United States, would that be a victory? I think so. And so did they. There will be a 50 percent reduction in crime for the next five years dropping another 10 percent after that leveling at 40 percent. Fifty percent drop in crime. I can live with that. We can all live with that. That sounds like a good deal. They thought so too. So I will live in La Jolla, and my wife, she's going to be involved in the arts. Did you know she used to be a *telenovela* star in Mexico? She's going to do a glamorous production of *Death of a Salesman*. She's going to look incredible. She's getting an herbal wrap today. Everything is looking good. I love the arts. I love this country better than anyone I know. *(Beat) Death of a Salesman.* Yes, *Death of a Salesman.* Ironic no? Well, it's going to be a hit. I guarantee it.

(Lights change. BUFORD GOMEZ and INEZ stand looking over a sunrise.)

BUFORD GOMEZ: I'm home in my own yard in the United States. I could kiss the ground, but I'm worried about the dog doodoo.

INEZ: You feeling okay honey?

BUFORD GOMEZ: Sure baby, I just been standing here looking at the lights—sun's coming up. *(Beat)* I been thinking, really thinking.

INEZ: Oh baby, you know how you hate doing that, come to bed.

BUFORD GOMEZ: This all has changed me. I'm going to take an early retirement. You know we could live in San Felipe, Mexico. A whole lot of Americans are doing that. The Mexicans are complaining we're taking it over. It's cheap there. We could have a satellite and a big screen TV. We'd be right on the border near everything.

INEZ: Sure baby, whatever you think is best as long as I say so. Your mother's been listening to a psychic who said she should try to travel.

BUFORD GOMEZ: Psychics don't work. They found one dead near the Del Mar racetrack. It was a mob hit. He should've seen it coming. He was a psychic.

(INEZ holds up a photograph.)

INEZ: Look. He's going to be big boy, look at the ultra sound.

BUFORD GOMEZ: I thought that was his arm.

INEZ: He's a Gomez man for sure. Your mother wants to name him Conception, after that *vaquero* who attacked them cartel boys.

BUFORD GOMEZ: Yeah, I know. I can't figure her out why she loves that name. Conception, I guess it means birth or life. They're going to nickname him Connie, he's going to grow up and be gay.

INEZ: She's been moping around wearing black. I think San Felipe will be good for her. The drug lord's dead so we'll be safe. You saw them kill him right?

BUFORD GOMEZ: I think so, that's what the FBI agent I saw said after the hypnotism debriefing thing they did on me. It's in the report. Although they did lose some files, but they said they weren't important.

INEZ: San Felipe Mexico, it's on the border near the ocean right?

BUFORD GOMEZ: Uhmmm. Think of it honey, me living in Mexico. There's an irony in that but I just can't seem to see it.

INEZ: You never do honey.

(Lights flicker.)

INEZ: That's strange. You notice that lately. The lights flickering, the cold draft. Sometimes I swear there's a ghost here.

BUFORD GOMEZ: Yeah, I always feel I'm being watched in the shower.

INEZ: Come to bed.

BUFORD GOMEZ: You know I did a lot of thinking in that cell and maybe this border that I swore to protect it's just a line, a symbol. I think the border is something we share. We share each side of it. It's not a line that divides us. It's alive, it's breathing and it can't be something that divides us. It's got to be something we both share . . . Aww, damn, I got a headache.

INEZ: Come to bed baby, it's almost dawn.

BUFORD GOMEZ: Yeah, I see the sun coming up. It's gonna be a new day, a new day for all of us.

(The stage lights brighten mimicking a sunrise. Then suddenly they go black.)

The End

Photo by Susie Albin-Najera

*Following a performance of **Buford Gomez**, Rick L. Najera (c.) and Rene Lavan are interviewed by the media.*

RICK L. NAJERA

"Poet and producer, actor and comedian, award-winning TV writer, denizen of the Latin quarter, Hollywood Hills and Great White Way, Rick Najera is the embodiment of diversity."

—Writers Guild of America

Rick L. Najera is an award-winning actor-writer-director-producer with credits in film, television, theatre and Broadway. Honored twice by *Hispanic Business Magazine* as one of the "100 Most Influential Latinos in America," Najera is one of the most powerful voices in the Latino world today.

With an extensive range of talent, Najera has enjoyed working in many forms of entertainment, whether writing for television or film to acting and theatrical stage performance.

He has starred and guest starred in numerous TV shows and films and developed original sketch comedy for TV, stage and Internet.

Najera penned the holiday feature film *Nothing Like the Holidays*, starring Debra Messing, Alfred Molina and John Leguizamo, which won him a prestigious ALMA Award. He was also honored with two WGA nominations for his writing on MAD TV.

His writing/acting credits also include the critically acclaimed, award-winning stage works, *Latinologues™* (Broadway), directed by Cheech Marin; an interactive, musical comedy *Sweet 15–Quinceañera*; and *Diary of a Dad Man*, which premiered on *Showtime* in January 2011 as a half-hour comedy special that he wrote, executive produced and starred in. His next comedy special, *Legally Brown* also aired on *Showtime* in 2011.

Najera has also written for groundbreaking television comedies such as *MAD TV*, *In Living Color* and Culture Clash.

As one of the only three Latinos in history to write and star in his own show on Broadway, Najera made his Broadway debut in 2005 with his self-written and created, award-winning sketch comedy show, *Latinologues*™. The show triumphed on Broadway at the historic Helen Hayes Theatre on W. 44 Street for a four-month run (137 performances with an extension), a historical achievement for a Latino-oriented show. Najera's show on Broadway paved the way for other acts to follow such as Tony Award winning, *In The Heights*. With a more than 15-year history of performances, *Latinologues* has toured the nation to sold-out houses and standing ovations. *Latinologues* is the longest-running and only showcase of its kind for Latinos in America, and Najera has mentored and directed more than 150 actors in the show.

Najera's other works include, *Latins Anonymous, A Peculiar People, A Quiet Love* and *The Pain of the Macho.*

Curtain call for Latinologues *at the Ricardo Montalban Theatre in Los Angeles.*

Photo by Susie Albin-Najera

ACKNOWLEDGMENTS

Special thanks to those who helped in the making of this book and for making *Latinologues* possible:

Mary and Edward Najera, Robin Tate, Sam Woodhouse, Susie Albin-Najera, Cheech Marin, Geraldo Rivera, Luis Alberto Urrea, Tavis Smiley, Rene Lavan, Jacob Vargas, Tony Plana, Scott Montoya, Elena Sotomayor, Henry Cardenas, Fernando Carrillo, Kevin Benson, Rafael Agustin, Oscar Toruno, Momo Rodriguez, Eric Roberts, Dominic Vicari, Juan Carlos Zapata, Jim McNamara, Rosalinda Morales, Ted Perkins, David Ames, Bel Hernandez, Lisa Zion, Priscilla Gonzalez Sainz, Lucia Zepeta, Jesse Garcia, Eugenio Derbez, Mike Najera, Luis Raul, Matilda Toledo, Rudy Moreno, Carlos Gomez, Emilio Rivera, Yareli Arizmendi, Sergio Arau, Cynthia Klitbo, Jaime Camil, Katie Barberi, Gabriel Gonzales, Art Rutter, Chingo Bling, Angelo Collado, Abeladro de la Peña Jr. , Alan Mercer, Santiago, Carmen Hernandez, Alia Taraf, Raul de Molina, Luis Balaguer, Mario Bosquez, Barry Kearson, Jose Marquez, Carmen Guevarra, Daniel Hastings, Gary Blumsack, Danna Hyams, Dawn Page, Dyana Ortelli, Lupe Ontiveros, Jimmy Smits, Maria Conchita Alonso, Fidel Arizmendi, Reyna Trevino, Fred and Linda Sotelo, Alex Montoya, Hengee, David Salzman, Idalis de Leon, Idalys Garcia, Sergio Aguerro, Beth Sullivan, Frank Carbajal, Jeremy Berry, Josh Norek, Kiki Melendez, Lara Tal, Fern Ornstein, Lidia Martinez, Marco Rodriguez, Miranda Martinez, Paul Murad, Pat Buckley, Gene Pompa, Yvonne de la Rosa, Xavier the X Man, Manny Ruiz, Mike Robles, Chris Nunley, Jay Torres, Chunky Sanchez, Trina Bardusco, Paul Saucido, Steven T. Seagle, Kirk Whisler, Katharine A. Díaz, and all of the cast and crew for the past 15 or more years.

For a sample list of performers throughout the years, visit: www.latinologues.net.

Special thanks to Julian, Sonora and Kennedy, the three best productions in my life.

WORDS FROM COLLEAGUES & PEERS

I remember an acting coach telling me to use a comedic monologue from a book entitled Latins Anonymous, *by Rick Najera. I read the book and was an immediate fan carrying the book with me religiously. A month or so later I was invited to a play entitled* Latinologues *on Broadway. After the show I was invited to meet the cast and the writer who—unbeknownst to me—was Rick Najera. Rick was so unbelievably kind and forthcoming with all of his experience and knowledge. He signed my book and several years later I had the extreme honor of working with him in the very play I saw on Broadway. I will be forever grateful for the experience and the opportunity Rick presented me with. He's hilarious, honorable, talented and real.*

—Jackie Quiñones, actress/producer

Latinologues *is a comedy written by a Latino for Latinos. In times where Latinos in the industry are at an all time low; especially when you examine film, TV, radio and theater. Where is the next Latino Tyler Perry? Where are the Latino comedy writers? America and Hollywood, please take note: Rick Najera is here. He's been here and he's here to stay.*

—Oskar Toruno, producer/writer/actor

I jumped at the chance to be involved with Latinologues *because I believe it to be a clever funny show that's well written and beautifully executed. I also believe Rick Najera to be a white guy pretending to be Latino. Either way, he's extremely talented!*

—Douglas Spain, actor (including *Band of Brothers*)

[Rick Najera] simply understands what it means to be a Latino trying to find his place in the American culture, and he says it better and funnier than anyone else I've seen try. Rick Najera is truly a pioneer of a people who need to be heard.

—Katie Barberi, *telenovela* actress (including *Doña Bárbara*)

The key to seeing more Latinos on TV and film is to have more writers like Rick. Humor is a very powerful tool and when a culture is able to make fun of itself, it shows that it's part of the social fabric of society.

—Aimee Garcia, actress, *Spanglish* and series regular on *Dexter, Trauma* and the *George Lopez Show*

More Opportunities

Latino Print Network, WPR BOOKS sister organization, works with over 625 Hispanic newspapers and magazines. These publications have a combined circulation of 19 million in 177 markets nationwide.

Latino Literacy Now is a 501(c)3 organization that has produced 48 **Latino Book & Family Festivals** around the USA since it's founding in 1997. Over 800,000 people have attended these events. It also has carried out the **International Latino Book Awards** since 1997 and the **Latino Book into Movies Awards** since 2010.

Hispanic Marketing 101 is a twice-weekly eNewsletter that provides a variety of helpful information. A subscription is free at **www. HM101.com** We have these and other programs that may be of interest to you.